When Wanderers
Cease to Roam

When Wanderers Cease to Roam

A Traveler's Journal of Staying Put

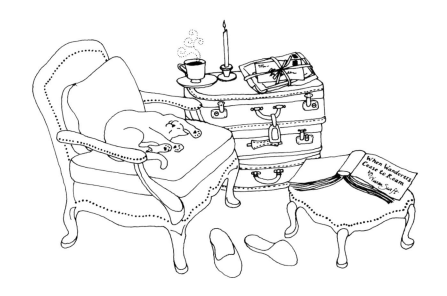

Vivian Swift

BLOOMSBURY

Published by Bloomsbury USA, New York.

All papers used by Bloomsbury USA are natural, recyclable products made from wood grown in well-managed forests. The manufacturing processes conform to the environmental regulations of the country of origin.

LIBRARY OF CONGRESS CATALOGING-IN-PUBLICATION DATA HAS BEEN APPLIED FOR.

ISBN-10 1-59691-461-0
ISBN-13 978-1-59691-461-2

First U.S. Edition 2008

1 3 5 7 9 10 8 6 4 2

The entire text of this book has been hand lettered by the author.
Printed in China by RR Donnelley, South China Printing Co. Ltd.

DEDICATED
to
WALTER MARLIN
Road Builder of Edinburgh
Being famous for paving the Royal Mile for King James V in 1532,
Walter Marlin's last wish was to be buried under the cobblestones
of his *own* road there, **Marlin's Wynd.**

I get that.
Life is short. The road is forever.

And
to my Mother
MARY MARLIN
Thanks for the DNA

My profound gratitude goes to Maggie Klein, Editor and Publisher of the best newspaper in Westchester County, New York, **The Pelham Weekly**, for her gracious permission to reprint news articles. Although the language and content of the articles have been preserved, names and identifying information have been changed to protect individuals' privacy.

To the University of Chicago Press, acknowledgement is made for their permission to reprint the last two lines from Joseph P. Clancy's translation of "Ode I·6" from his *Horace Odes and Epodes,* ©1960 by The University of Chicago. All rights reserved.

Appreciation is given for the excerpts from *My Antonia* by Willa Cather, copyright 1918, 1926 by Willa Sibert Cather, renewed 1946 by Willa Sibert Cather; copyright © renewed 1954 by Edith Lewis. Reprinted by permission of Houghton Mifflin Company. All rights reserved.

To the estate of Barbara Pym, thankful acknowledgement is made for kind permission to reprint a line from her novel, *A Glass of Blessings,* E.P. Dutton, ©1959, ©1980.

Grateful acknowledgement is made to The Millay Society for permission to reprint two lines lines from "Winter Night" by Edna St. Vincent Millay. Copyright 1928 by Edna St. Vincent Millay and Norma Millay Ellis.

January

Winter Mind

JANUARY is the Warrior Month because it takes a **WARRIOR** to soldier through these cold, dark, harsh January days. This must be why the Romans put January at the head of the calendar, the better to teach the most important lesson of the year, that:

What it takes
to get through January
is what it takes
to get through **LIFE**.

IT TAKES a *Winter Mind*

Before I got my Winter Mind only **Summer** mattered to me. Summer was the significant season, the time to:

Run away to Paris for the first time,
Follow the midnight sun to Loch Ness,
Dance in the moonlight in Buenos Aires,
Hitch hike across the Holy Land,
Swim in the Trevi after dark,
Trek up the Niger, hunker down for tea time
      with nomads in the Sahara,
Kneel in the shadows of the Sarsen Circle
      at Stonehenge,
Chase the spirit of "The Wanderer Queen"
      all the way to Carthage.

Then I came to live in this little Village on the Long Island Sound and I discovered my **Winter Mind** and with it *I discovered the rest of the year.*

10 **Winters** is what I'm talking about 〜 10 Summers, Springs, and Falls too. Whenever I would wonder **Where do I go now?** the only good answer was: **Don't go. Stay put.** And every month there was a good reason to do just that.

In JANUARY I stayed because of my **Winter Mind**.

January 1

January, the Warrior month – this will be the 10th Winter I've soldiered through in this cold little Village. Why have I stayed in one place so long? Could be because all the while I tried to think of somewhere else to go – somewhere **unusual** and **busy** – all my new furniture and all my old memories were fitting in perfectly *here*.

Who I used to be, and who I always wanted to be, seemed comfortable together in this quiet little Village on the Long Island Sound, and that's as good a reason to stay put as any.

January 7

Coldest January in 10 years. I put on my very warm & very ugly Winter coat and I put two mittens on each hand and I walked out of the Village today, down to the Sound. To see for myself if the stories were true, that the sea had frozen. And **YES** it had! The Sound is an icy inlet, as smooth as a skating pond. The waves were caught by the freeze and turned into a thick fringe of frosty lace on the rocky shore.

January 12

SUN SET at 4:30 PM today. The shadows of the late afternoon on the snow turn it into the thousand shades of blue that you don't see at any other time of year.

January 13

Another ordinary, breathtaking Winter color: Cardinal red *right out my bedroom window.* No wonder I want to stay put right here.

January 17

My birthday was yesterday. So today I had my favorite breakfast of the year: LEFT-OVER BIRTHDAY CAKE IN BED. Rain and ice beat at the windows, but I had five cats and two quilts to keep me warm.

January 20

More rain and ice – plus snow and wind – what the weatherman calls A WINTERY MIX of MESSY WEATHER. I ventured into the Village on errands and in ten minutes there were icicles on my umbrella. Just think: in Rio de Janeiro it's the middle of **Summer.**

January 22

Snow all day, blowing into drifts against the Village like the incoming tide of an ice-age sea.

January 25

Ice storm today, battering against every window in the house. Even the cats were disturbed, woken from their naps by the din of pounding wind rattling all the panes of glass.

JANUARY 27 is the day of MAXIMUM COOLING,

the day of the mathematical calculation for when the Northern Hemisphere has lost its last trace of residual heat from last summer. But it was mild today – the typical January thaw of a day or two. Sea gulls from the Long Island Sound swooped inland, flocking to the air above the Village, flying and swirling in the hundreds, celebrating their wings and their joy at being sea gulls.

January 29

Severe wind chill and frostbite warnings are back in the news today, so the schools closed for a Snow Day. I went out anyway, for the same reason I once walked into a Sahara sandstorm, and alongside a Kentucky tornado. It was fun!

January 31

Sleet, then a blizzard of snow in a 30-knot gale. In the back yard the little brown birds took shelter in the bare bushes, huddling in their tiny feathers, waiting out January.

HOW TO *Winterize* your MIND

ONE : See the sun rise and set every day.
The average night is 13½ hours long.
We spend most of January in the dark.
Don't miss a minute of daylight.

two : Learn how to draw a tree.
Now is the best time to see what a tree
REALLY looks like. Draw one a day.

three : Put something beautiful in your
room so that it's the first thing that
you see when you wake up.

an aqua-colored princess phone
an antique perfume bottle
a glass wind chime
a Spode tea cup, a tin of Assam tea
a blue jay feather
the words to your favorite song
a puddle of Summer rain

The truth about January

LONG AGO in December **52** BCE a Roman General
LUCIUS POSTUMIUS ALBINUS wanted to declare
WAR in Spain. However, ANCIENT TRADITION was
that ALL Roman wars began on the NEW YEAR
in *MARCH* which is why MARCH was named for
MARS the *GOD* of *WAR*. SO the General
simply moved the NEW YEAR to JANUARY and marched
to Spain and for over TWO THOUSAND YEARS no one
has had the guts to move it **back** where it belongs.

four : Mend something.
With your hands
Sew it, glue it, nail it, FIX IT.

five : Seahorses, ladybugs,
woolly bear caterpillars,
and dragonflies do it –
HIBERNATE.
Life is but a Winter Dream.

Scenes from a SNOW DAY

Snowmen DAYDREAMING

MAKING SNOW ANGELS

SHOWING OFF

Snowmen DIVING

DOING LAPS

SYNCHRONIZED SWIMMING

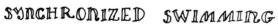

The *Lone Skater* and other scenes from the *LONG ISLAND SOUND*

A **SOUND** is a body of water that is almost entirely surrounded by land.

The **LONG ISLAND SOUND** is 110 miles long and has a maximum width of 21 miles.

The Sound has a 600-mile-long coastline along the states of NEW YORK, RHODE ISLAND & CONNECTICUT.

HERE IS WHERE I LIVE

The LONG ISLAND SOUND

CONNECTICUT

NEW YORK

RHODE ISLAND

ATLANTIC OCEAN

Tides from the Atlantic Ocean tear into an eastern entrance of the Sound called *The RACE* and rip out of a western exit called *The HELLGATE.*

There are 20 million people living within 40 miles of the Long Island Sound but because of its ragged coastline a person needs only to walk 5 minutes to find a hidden bay, a secret backwater, an old harbor, or a deserted beach in complete isolation.

SMALL PLEASURES
worth staying HOME for

A local museum has a collection of sea creatures from the waters of the Long Island Sound. In a special aquarium there, a herd of **SEA HORSES** hibernates.

In their simulated habitat, the sea horses cluster around each other. Each sea horse's tail is coiled around a blade of seaweed - their anchors in the gently flowing water. This keeps the herd from floating apart. Their eyes are closed, unaware that they are on exhibit. Some of the sea horses are slumbering with their tiny muzzles resting on their little chests. Other sea horses snooze with heads leaning to one side, on an invisible watery pillow. Together they bob in the water, in the flow of the simulated sea current. They sleep on and on, dreaming their January dreams.

Sipping a cup of **LAPSANG SOUCHONG** tea
that tastes like *January*
DEEP · DARK · BITTER
Like smoke from an ancient fire

A Blizzard Big fistfuls of snow falling from the sky for **10 hours** ∽ **Beautiful** and **terrible**, but mostly *BEAUTIFUL*.

REMEMBERING *blue birds* and warmer days:
a **Kingfisher** on **KEY WEST**
an **ABYSSINIAN ROLLER** on the **SAHARA**
PEACOCKS in the **JORDAN VALLEY**

Sewing in the company of a Cat

Humming a sad song on a solitary walk on a cold day ∽ but not feeling **sad**.

A BIRTHDAY MEMOIR

in Five Minuscule Chapters

1. On the banks of the Niger River in one of the hottest countries on Earth, sharing Emmenthaler and Grand Marnier with half a dozen scruffy Peace Corps Volunteers. I am 25 and this is the first time I've worn a summer dress on my BIRTHDAY.

2. Celebrating at the King David Hotel (built in 1931) in Jerusalem (founded in 2000 BCE) where the *tomates provençals* are unforgettable and I have no idea that my soldier dining companion will become my first husband. I am 30.

3. One for the Wheel of Life: "Pierre", the worst boyfriend **EVER**, keeps my mind off my job, the worst job *ever* (retail sales of discount jewelry). I'm about a year away from my big career break (million-dollar jewels) and my first date with a new fiancé, but for now, my 35th is the worst birthday <u>ever</u>.

4. On a get-away weekend to the Long Island Sound I'm given antique jingle bells. "Just until you choose your RING," he says. I'm turning 37 and I don't get it. Then he proposed.

5. Un-engaged, back on the Sound, one minute past midnight, a knock on my door. "I couldn't wait to see what you look like now that you're 40!" he says, offering me a bottle of champagne and a copy of Jabberwocky. This was our 2ND date. It was the next-to-last one, too ∿ and by then I'd decided that **STAYING PUT** was my kind of place.

next page

MINDFULNESS and MITTENS
Tiny baby-size mittens, lost and scattered in the snow. One by one, year after year, I picked them up. **TEN YEARS**. I can't show you my Winter Mind but I *can* show you 19 found mittens.

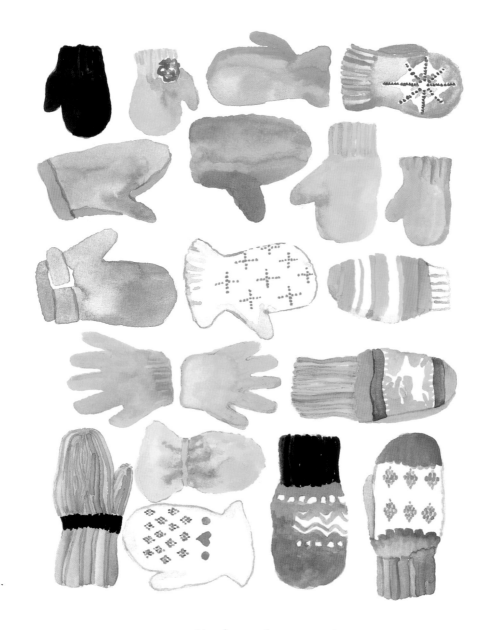

all those lost mittens

SNOWFALL all night, and then an evil rain all day ⁓ rain full of little spears of ice. I had no reason to set foot out of doors so I sat by my window and watched the little brown birds withstand all that weather, four brave birds I named

ENDURANCE, Patience, Bug, & FAITH

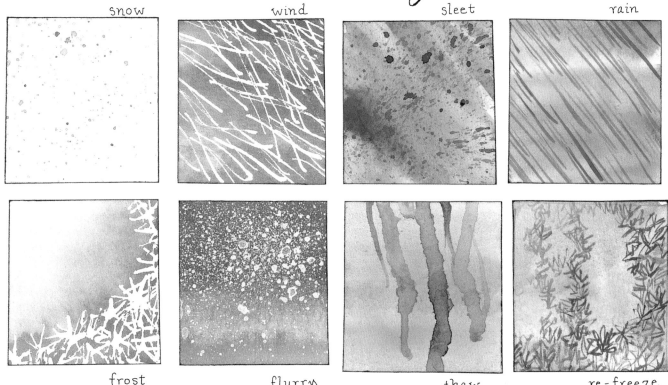

snow

wind

sleet

rain

frost

flurry

thaw

re-freeze

Strong · Tough · Fearless

Winter Gulls are found in large flocks on the seasides of America from Maine to Florida. In flight the birds are as mesmerizing as the breaking waves on the shores below.

ON a rare day of JANUARY THAW sea gulls give in to their urge to REJOICE

Winter Coats

The **STOAT** is a brown weasel. In WINTER the animal's fur turns pure white except for the tip of its tail and is known as **ERMINE**

This:

is the luxurious pelt used to trim the robes and gowns of **ROYALTY**

THINGS THAT KEEP YOU WARM in JANUARY

Hot chocolate, ice cold champagne. Not in the same glass, but in the same afternoon.

A window shopping trip to browse for a new piece of jewelry (rubies and peridots feel very warm this time of year).

The Old Boyfriend Sweater, the one that good-old-what's-his-name didn't even know you kept after you broke up with him.

ODE to my WINTER COAT

You've been my **coat** for so many years
With you I've had no Winter fears

You're the best coat I ever wore
I'll crave for fashion **NEVERMORE**

O How I love you, **Winter Coat,**
Even tho you are the color of **STOAT**

I was born and raised inland. That's why there's hardly a beach anywhere in the world — the Riviera, California, Brazil, North Africa, Mexico — that doesn't bore me after a day or two. Because compared to the complicated, interesting geography of the woods and mountains where I grew up, a beach (flat, wide, plain) doesn't have much *there* there.

But then I came to live on the Long Island Sound. Here is a coast that has no straight lines and all the moods and wilderness of an old growth forest. For every **one** mile that the sea gull here flies across the water's edge, there are **six** miles of jagged, twisting shore on the ground. I can wander these beaches forever.

Winter Whites

Job Interviews
First Dates
Author's Photos

I want to keep this white turtleneck sweater with the black racing stripes on the sleeves until I'm 100 years old. So I save it for special ocassions, wearing it once or twice a year, only for the times I want to look extra-spiffy.

I also **love** this skirt and it doesn't even look **good** on me. It's a hiphugger style and it's made of wool, so it's very bulky. But it's got my two essentials for **fabulousness**, really cool zippers and great-looking pockets.

When I wear this outfit I feel like I'm a hip, off-duty stewardess from the 1960s.

Horace,
King of the seagulls

"Three Ducks Up The Wallish"

I was in awe of English accents — it was my first journey around Britain and I was an eager audience for any native speaker. Tea time at the Canterbury Youth Hostel, a girl from London was filling me in on anarchy in the U.K. 1976: "The royal family," she sneered, one world-weary 20-year-old to another, "is *so* **three ducks up the wallish.**"

First produced in the 1930s, cheap Staffordshire ceramic bird decorations became ubiquitous in the decor of working class households, a pretension to middle class gentrification much despised by intellectuals and non-conformists.

But by the 1990s these gee-gaws had become highly ironic, and highly collectible — Notting Hill antiques shops were selling them for £200.

In the window of an antiques shop in the Village I spied a set **marked down.** Vintage Beswick ducks (actually, they were *terns*) weren't as ironic on the Long Island Sound as they were in London. I bought my first set for $18.00.

Now I have over 40 birds in my living room, flying up my wallish in flocks of ducks, geese, pheasants, and especially **SEA GULLS.** Nobody *gets it.* Not even me, anymore. I've laid my irony to **REST.**

Winter Mind

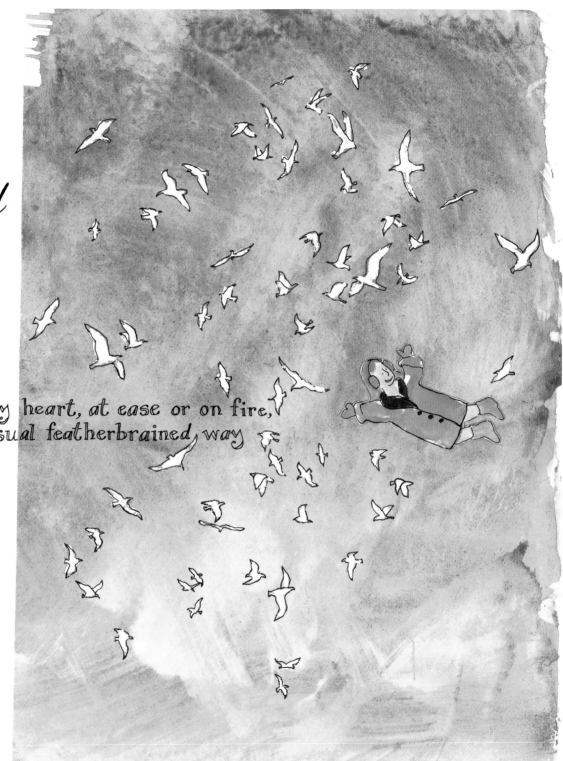

Celebrating my heart, at ease or on fire,
in my usual featherbrained way

Horace, Roman poet
Ode I·6 , 23 BCE

February

FEBRUARY is not dull!
Not when the Village newspaper is chock full of *fascinating* items about Village life:

THE WEEKLY NEWS

Miss Bev Celebrating 47th Year

Miss Bev, owner of the Village Dance Studio, is celebrating her 47th year in business. Miss Bev was a professional dancer who left the performance arena of the profession to follow her dream of teaching.

One of Miss Bev's ballet students.

Swan Crosses Fifth Avenue

A swan walked across Fifth Avenue in the Village on Valentine's Day and was accidentally hit by a car. Police and fire units responded. The injured swan was put in a dog carrier and then taken to a near-by wildlife rehabilitator.

Shrub Taken, Found

Village Police investigated the theft of a 5ft. shrub that was stolen from a house on Willowdale Ave. Later the property was found and returned to the owner.

Women's Club Holds Benefit Highlighting Frank Sinatra's Career in Film

Have You Heard?

Just how many individual residents have signed up for the Village Public Library card? The count is now over 7,000!

But February *is* an
ACQUIRED TASTE

February used to be the month I paid the least attention to, except as inspiration to plan a long road trip as far away as possible.

Now that I've acquired the habit of staying put, February is the month that keeps me closest to home, feasting on the memories of travel and news of my neighbors.

February 2
MID-WINTER DAY
The snow is old and dirty and the sun did not peep through heavy grey clouds all day. The reason to collect bright memories is for days like this.

February 3
Another blizzard. Then drenching rain. Then snow again. That's a whole lot of Winter in one day.

February 5
Big story in the Village newspaper: a white squirrel was spotted on 3rd Ave. And there's going to be a lecture on the history of paperweights for the off-season meeting of the Garden Club.

February 8
Warmer temperatures overnight. This break in the weather brings the skunks out. I came across a skunk this morning, browsing through my neighbor's trash. The *skunk*, that is (not me), was browsing, looking for leftover cat food. *Me,* I'm browsing through all my bright memories.

February 10
Today is the coldest day of the year – *9°.* I took the opportunity to go outside to blow soap bubbles, to see if such bubbles freeze instantly when it's this cold (they do) and if they make a sound when they break (none that I could hear).

February 13
Blizzard alert. We could be snowed in for days. *DAYS.* I have just the project to keep me happy if I'm going to be snow-bound indoors: I'm going to illustrate all my old travel diaries and make lots of toast.

February 14
Atmospheric conditions are similar to those that produce thunderstorms in the Summer today but, this being February and frigid, there is only a ring around the moon tonight, an optical illusion from all that lightning in the air frozen into a ring of silent thunder.

February 17
Item in the Village newspaper: Today is the 100th day of school. The kindergartners made 100 Day hats and told stories about what life will be like when they are 100.

February 20
The Main Street has been cleared as a one-lane road by a solitary snow plow. I didn't meet another soul on my walk into town today except for an orange balloon that blew in from nowhere. It tumbled past me like a happy traveler, down the middle of the street. Later I saw the same balloon caught high in the bare branches of the old tree on the corner of my lane, waving in the wind. I named him SPUTNIK.

February 23
HALF WAY through the last half of Winter.

February 27
Today the snow melted and revealed a parched Earth – yellow grass lawns, cinders and dead leaves like straw everywhere. I've read that the GOBI looks like this, our February desert.

February 28
Last night I dreamt that I was flying like a bird over Zanzibar. I've never been to Zanzibar. In fact, I've never been to any country that starts with a Z. It is February, and I have Zanzibar on my mind.

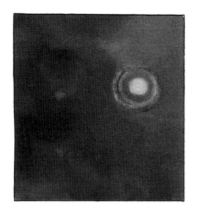

February 14
Electrons in a ring
around the moon

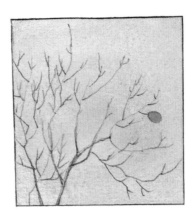

February 20
Sputnik in a small world

February 28
Zanzibar in a dream

The Taste of February

CINNAMON TOAST DELUXE

1-pound loaf fresh white bread
1 cup butter
1 cup fine granulated sugar
2 tablespoons ground cinnamon

Cut slices of bread diagonally. Heat butter in frying pan and sauté slices slowly, 2 or 3 at a time, adding butter until each piece is golden-brown on each side, but not dark. Remove slices from skillet and drop into a clean brown paper bag containing a mixture of sugar and cinnamon. Shake gently and serve warm. Makes 24 to 32 pieces.

note: For variety, combine sugar and cinnamon and a little water to make a paste. Dip bread into paste and sauté in butter until browned. The sugar and butter will caramelize and give the toast a delicious crisp crust. Serve hot.

CARAMEL ~ CARDAMOM TOAST

16 slices of bread
1 cup firmly packed brown sugar
½ cup butter
¼ teaspoon ground cardamom

Toast bread on one side, remove crusts. Spread untoasted side generously with mixture of the remaining ingredients. Toast this side under broiler until bubbly and brown. Cut into fingers before serving.

HONEY ALMOND TEA TOAST

Spread white bread with butter, then with honey. Sprinkle with sliced almonds and broil until browned. Delicious with afternoon tea.

Take the worst day you had in *JANUARY*

REPEAT 28 TIMES

That's **FEBRUARY**

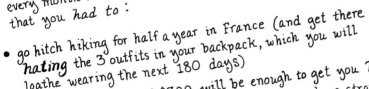

These are the days for remembering when FEBRUARY made you stir crazy~~ You were in your 20s and so eager to make your life INTERESTING and *complicated* every month of the year, and February was SO DULL, that you *had* to:

- go hitch hiking for half a year in France (and get there **hating** the 3 outfits in your backpack, which you will loathe wearing the next 180 days)

- hope your budget of $300 will be enough to get you *THERE* (which is anywhere not HERE) and back (but you end up stranded in Rome, where older, richer tourists will take pity on you while you wait and *wait* for a wire from home and stuff thousands of liras into your pitiful hands at the Leonardo da Vinci airport)

- join the PEACE CORPS (so you will ever after remember when there was a time that there were places on Earth **so far away** that you were sent to live in a country that NO ONE had ever HEARD of)

Passport Photo, 1975
Not valid in CUBA NORTH KOREA
NORTH VIET-NAM

Me
and my first passport

1975

I think that I am like a lot of people my age who consider themselves *world travelers*. My generation, after all, made **TRAVEL** what it is today, when we went *abroad* in droves in the 1970s. And I actually called it that: *ABROAD*. I quit jobs and schools and boyfriends to go *abroad*.

Back in the 1970s jet travel was still new & exciting. In 1978, my heyday, only 17% of Americans had ever *been on a plane*. **I**, and a few ten thousand others my age, changed *that* by herding ourselves off to Europe, each of us *travelers* in the most thrilling, $10-A-Day sense of the word.

Today 84% of Americans fly at least once a year. Today, it's hard to remember when getting on a plane was an exciting event, when *abroad* was truly *FAR, FAR AWAY*.

I became a new being and the subject of my own admiration. I was a traveler! A word never tasted so good in my mouth before.

Mark Twain, on his first trip away from home, down the Mississippi River

Me
after *Paris*
UTTERLY
SOPHISTICATED

But **TRAVEL** these days means something completely different. It's just something that people put in their Personal Ads to make themselves sound interesting. These days, it's a **family vacation** in Bali, it's **e-mailing** from Tierra del Fuego, it's **cell phoning** from Mt. Everest.

Travel is not what it used to be.
And that's a good reason to **STAY PUT.**

25

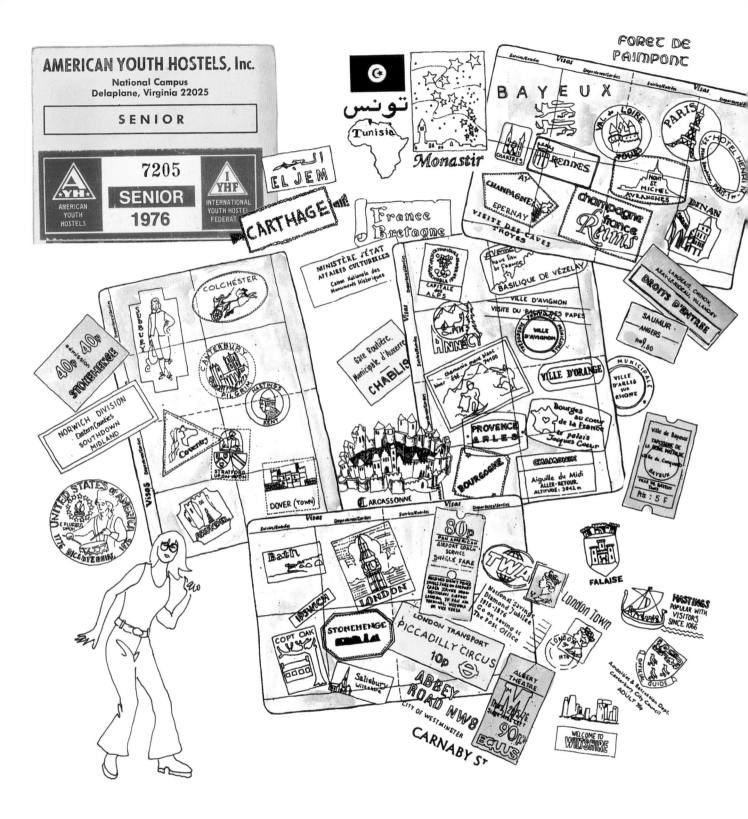

1977: **NO** Sex · Drugs Rock and Roll

Not for me. Sure, I saw Punks in London — hair sticking straight out of their heads, black face make up, ears/eyes/nose/lips pierced — they **scared** me.

So I lit out for **Ipswich** (see: Punch line, Dead Parrot sketch, Monty Python, c.1969). And, from there, on to Bury St. Edmunds, Copt Oak, and Colchester, places so obscure that no normal 21-year-old would cross a **street**, let alone an **ocean**, for.

All I can say for myself is that I was trying my best **not** to be such a **hick**, but I was neither angry nor middle-class enough to endorse anarchy in the U.K.

So I was **very** pleased with myself when I went to Paris and met a boy from California and let him kiss me on Bastille Day. We were up all night, roaming from one boozy street party to another, drunk on our certainty that here was proof positive (in the dawn's light) that we were not going to be anything at all like our parents when we grew up.

Here's how we turned out: The boy from California went home and became a lawyer. He got married. I've settled down in my Village, still working at entry-level jobs. He has 2 kids. I have 5 cats. He and his family wear matching outfits for their Xmas card pictures. I've heard the little girl next door call me "the Cat Lady". Our 21-year-old selves would **hate** us.

DISCO 1978

London

TAVISTOCK

DEVON

Salisbury

Clovelly

CORNWALL

TINTAGEL

Exmoor Ponies

Skye

Glasgow

LOCH LOMOND

loch ness

Scotland
purple heather & golden eagles

Monte Carlo

NORMANDIE BAYEUX FRANCE

Quimper

OMAHA BEACH

MontBlanc

hennebont Quimperlé roncarneau

Pont Aven

Chartres

BRETAGNE

St MALO

Le MONT St MICHEL

PLANTAGENET

fédération unie des auberges de jeunesse

CARTE D'ADHÉRENT
1979
valable jusqu'au 31 décembre

YHF
INTERNATIONAL YOUTH
HOSTEL FEDERATION

N° 027848

Fly
AIR FRANCE

12 07 9 35 9 9 7
10 00 023.00

TARIF

PARIS MONTPARNASSE

CHARTRES

0800
Classe 2

89 km

Vivian,
cher ballon,

Je t'embrasse,
et attends ta venue
à bientôt

SNCF
PARIS AUST
TOURNEMIRE ROQUEFORT
départ
0807 1941

023.00 F
SNCF
PARIS
MONTPARNASSE
*
CHARTRES
SNCF classe
89 km

CARTE ORANGE
N° 6085347

coupon mensuel
zones de validité:

1 2

12 MAI 79

2 M 12

52 T

NIGER 1980-1982

REPUBLIQUE DU NIGER
TIMBRE TAXE POSTES
DE CROIX DE TAHOUA
50F

UNITED STATES OF AMERICA
PEACE CORPS
VOLUNTEER
ACTION FORM A-256
1980 - 1982
(1/73)
GPO 940-890

REPUBLIQUE DU NIGER
25F
GIRAFES
PROTECTION DE LA FAUNE

BAOBAB TREE

AFRICA

After the rainy season,
the thrilling sandstorms of the
HARMATTAN

A gift from Paris:
a bottle of lemon scent
EAU DE GUERLAIN

TEA CUPS the color of
AMBER

The sound of certain words:
QUOI
Quinine

And when I dream of
Africa: coeur

AIR AFRIQUE

29

MY LAST HITCH HIKE

At least once in your life shouldn't you buy a one-way ticket to a place you've *Never Seen?*

CONNEMARA
CONNAUGHT

Bíonn siúlach
scéalach

The traveller has tales to tell

LEINSTER

GAILLIMH

Dún na n Gall
Rossnowlagh

ANTRIM

ULSTER

WESTPORT

view of Dublin from my hotel room

Tea for One

every day café with my journal and my letters home

"There must be more to life than this,"

I said to myself one FEBRUARY: the weather was cold and grey, I hated my job as a salesgirl in the gift shop of a tourist hotel on Central Park South, I couldn't stand my boyfriend, and I was going to turn 30 on my next birthday.

IT WAS TIME TO DO SOMETHING DRASTIC.

So I bought a ONE WAY TICKET to IRELAND (I was a big U2 fan). My plan was to start in Galway and hitch hike around the world if I had to — if that's what it took to meet my FATE. I believed in fate. Because otherwise I'd have to believe in FEBRUARY.

Music for the
Last
Hitch Hike

a mix tape for the road
1985

WALKMAN

Heaven &
Ghost in You } Psychedelic
Furs

Hold Me Now - Thompson
Twins

Wake Me Up - Wham
Before You Go Go

Heart and Soul - T'Pau

Just Got Lucky - Jo
Boxer

Relax - Frankie Goes
To Hollywood

In a Big Country - Big
Country

Shout & - Tears for Fears
Everybody Wants
to Rule the World

Go Insane - Lindsay
Buckingham

Don't You Forget
About Me - Simple
Minds

Crazy For You - Madonna

Cruel Summer - Bananarama

Lawyers in Love - Jackson
Brown

The Heat is On - Glen Frey

Stand Back - Stevie Nicks

Don't Sleep in the
Subway Darling
Petula Clark

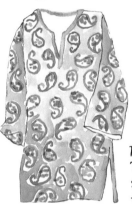

MY IRISH SUMMER

In Galway the average July temperature is 60° and it rains five times a day. The Irish say they have 40 words for rain, and I was rained on by them all, from fine misty rain to wet showers, to several kinds of downpours (cold, sudden, and/or continuous), to the most extreme **bucketing down** of rain. I had not packed for the chill and the damp so I had to buy this thick sweater on Day Two, at a shop whose woolens were so fresh off the sheep that my new sweater stank of lanolin. I reeked like a **barnyard** every time it got wet.

MASCOT
A stuffed koala I named Sandy Bear. Sometimes it made a good conversation piece and sometimes it made a good pillow.

MY PAISLEY MOOD
It would rain and my sweater would stink like sweaty mutton. I'd stand by the side of the road with my thumb out for *hours* GOING NOWHERE and the silent screaming in my head was deafening: *WHAT AM I DOING WITH MY LIFE?* Then the rain would end and a sympathetic Irish driver would stop his car for me and I'd be on my way to a far-away town that I'd never heard of. Later that evening, I'd be wearing this favorite Indian gauze blouse, listening to songs and stories told to me in West Country accents and it would occur to me that *This* is what I'm doing with my life.

A PERFECT FIT
The best jeans I ever wore, any time, any place.

FLOSS & NEEDLES

I sewed in train station waiting rooms and bus stop shelters. I sat & sewed on park benches on sunny days and more often I sat on my bed in dingy hotel rooms on rainy days and sewed. I sewed Gaelic alphabets and Celtic knots, and Irish dragons. They are all the souvenirs I have of Ireland.

P.S. I still have all this stuff, just in case.

On **EARTH**
it is not possible to be
more than
16,000 miles *from*
HOME

ZANZIBAR *on my mind*

The word for **TOURIST** in the Zanzibari language is derived from the verb **ZUNGUA** *meaning* To Go Around, To Turn, To Wander, *and* TO BE TIRESOME.

In 1831 a 22-year-old **CHARLES DARWIN** embarked on a 5-year journey around the world, **AFTER WHICH** he settled down in a London suburb and never set foot outside his homeland ever again.

As a young man, the scientist **ALEXANDER von HUMBOLDT** (1769-1859) spent 5 years in Latin America before settling down in Paris, where he spent **20** years writing **30** books about that one journey. HE ONLY RESUMED traveling in his 60th year, when he made a 9,000-mile trek through RUSSIA.

TODAY LUXURY CRUISE tourism on the **GALAPAGOS ISLANDS** is an $80-million-a-year business.

LE VOYAGE
PART IV
Charles Baudelaire, 1857

We saw the stars,
And the waves; we saw the sands, too.

And despite many shocks and unexpected disasters,
We were often bored JUST AS WE ARE HERE.

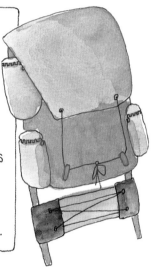

XAVIER de MAISTRE invented a new mode of travel in 1790 while under a 42-day house arrest for duelling:

ROOM TRAVEL.
He wrote an 80-page book, *Voyage Around My Room,* treating his furniture as major tourist attractions.

ROOM TRAVEL
is perfect for those without the wealth or courage to voyage around the world.

EASTER ISLAND
is where you **GO** to be the **FARTHEST** away from every other place in the **WORLD.**

Sundae Sunday

In a timely celebration 60 people enjoyed an "Ice Cream for Breakfast" party at the home of Dave and Millie Fitzpatrick last Sunday.

"There's nothing like shaking off the gloom of winter by waking up on the first Sunday of February and fixing a gooey sundae with whipped cream, hot fudge, nuts and a maraschino cherry," Dave said. P.S. at the party, the toppings seemed to disappear. Turns out that Cassie Ames was the pineapple thief and Timmy Heany ate all the gummy bears.

Displaying a valentine sent by the third graders at the Village Elementary School are some of the seniors at the Village Senior Citizens party.

Flour Sifter Taken

A flour sifter valued at $2.21 was shoplifted from the Shopping Center by a male wearing a cowboy hat. The Village Police were called to investigate and found a man matching the description in the parking lot. The man had the flour sifter in his possession and was charged with one count petit larceny.

St. Agnes Flea Market in Need of Donations

St. Agnes' Parish will be filled with treasures from furniture to valued collectibles at the Parish's Flea Market. Chairpersons Joyce C. and Laura Z. said they are overwhelmed with the generosity of Village residents and the wonderful assortment of donations thus far. They are still looking for more treasures which can be dropped off the Parish Center anytime.

School Selects School Pet

The Elementary School Student Government has been working on selecting a school pet. After a school-wide vote the winner was a chameleon. The students then researched the kinds of chameleons available, their needs, and costs. They also held a bake sale to raise funds for the purchase and maintenance of the pet. The successful bake sale allowed the students to purchase two chameleons.

Word is that we had 19.8 inches of snow in the Village from the Presidents Day Blizzard! With most people home for the holiday, the streets and roads were quiet and the snow fell and fell and fell. Several stores in downtown stayed closed for two days while the massive clean up and dig out began.

Groundhog Musical Gala Sunday, Feb. 7 2pm

No matter where you go, There you are.

march

MARCH

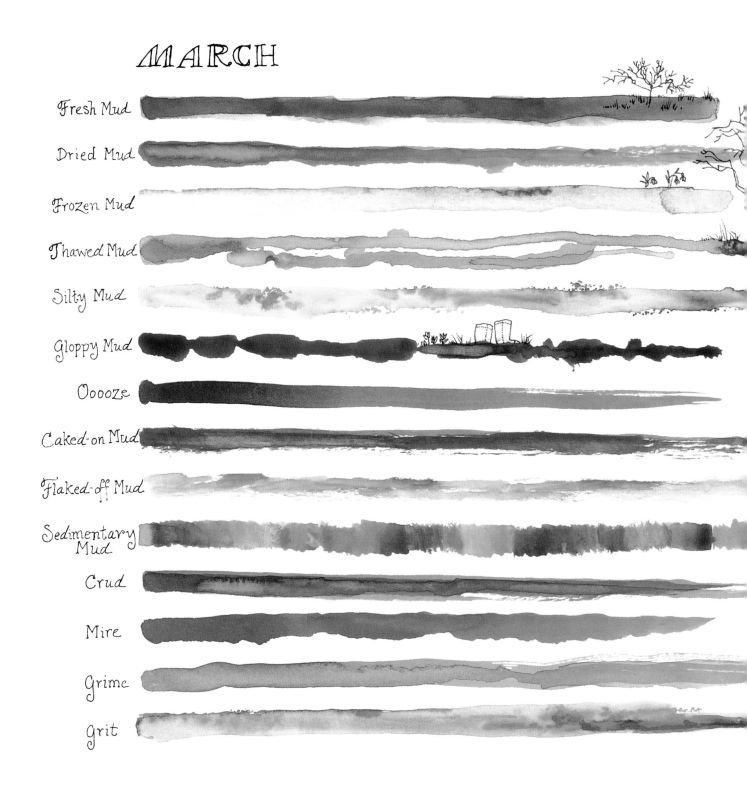

Fresh Mud

Dried Mud

Frozen Mud

Thawed Mud

Silty Mud

Gloppy Mud

Ooooze

Caked-on Mud

Flaked-off Mud

Sedimentary Mud

Crud

Mire

Grime

Grit

MARCH is the TEA TIME Month

When Life Gives You MARCH: make tea

Take the time to steep the leaves,
Stir in a long-lost flavor,
Serve it in a beautiful cup.
Restore your spirits in tiny sips of something warm and not-yet-forgotten.

POOR MARCH

It is the HOMELIEST month of the year. Most of it is MUD, EVERY IMAGINABLE FORM of MUD. AND what isn't MUD in March is ugly late-season SNOW falling onto the ground in filthy muddy heaps that look like PILES of DIRTY LAUNDRY.

MARCH

is the month in tatters, clothed in Winter rags, with *NOTHING* Spring-like to dress up in.

I didn't set out to collect teacups. I didn't intend to own 100 of them. But the Winters on the Long Island Sound are long and still and I have restless habits — a cup of tea settles and soothes and inspires a STAYING PUT kind of journey. Don't forget: Proust's *madeleine* was dipped into a cup of **TEA**.

The teacup **handle** was invented in England c. 1760

Handle
Grip
Hand-grip
Hold

Upper Terminal
Strap
Kick
Lower Terminal

Rim
Lip
Shoulder
Foot ring
Bowl

The **tea bowl** was invented in China c. 2737 BCE

Honey Cat at the open WINDOW gets a whiff of *MARCH*

March 3

On my doorstep this morning: a tea cup and saucer, with a note from my upstairs neighbor: *I know you like old china.*

March 3

The sky today is "Winter white"- it's blank, hazy, and dull. But it's much whiter than the acres of cruddy left-over snow everywhere.

March 6

I stayed indoors today and re-arranged my tea cup collection. I have as many tea cups as there are mornings, noons, and nights in March & that's how I'll get thru the last of Winter, by trying new teas in in each of my old tea cups.

March 10

The weather forecast was for *Late Winter Severe weather*. It was supposed to be a snow storm, but all we got was a hard cold rain. It made me brood all day, on the many ways I've missed my opportunities to do something useful and important with my life.

March 12

It snowed today. I made tea and sweetened it with Madagascar honey and suddenly I smelled the **flamboyants**, the scarlet flowers that bloom in the shade trees in Africa. Until today I had forgotten that I still remembered what it was like there, the shade and perfume of tea time in Africa.

March 17

I saw the First Robin today! He was bathing in a puddle of melted snow. I wanted to feel sorry for him because his puddle-bath was dirty and cold, but he was having too good a time flapping his wings and splashing in the water.

March 19

It's a bit milder today so I opened all the windows for the first time this year. The cats perched on the sills and inspected every breeze for good news from the outside world.

March 21

Slammed shut the windows today - it's *freezing* again.

March 24

A heavy rain and icy wind broke my umbrella today. I got soaked trudging home. I made some Irish Breakfast tea at 4:00pm and I got my broom and thumped on the ceiling to let my upstairs neighbor know he was invited to join me. We used my best Spode.

March 25

Five inches of snow fell last night. The first sound I heard this morning was the snow plow on the road in front of my house and birds singing. That's March for you— song birds and snow plows.

March 29

There is a little extra daylight at tea time this afternoon, an increase of 16 minutes already since the Spring equinox. This must be savored, so I made a pot of Earl Grey tea and remembered Buenos Aires.

March 31

This is the last day to see the crocuses in bloom, hundreds of them in a field on the edge of town. It's a spectacle ~ thousands of flower petals twinkling over the snow like a strange lavender mist. And to think that as a 16-year-old I had to hitch hike all the way to San Francisco for purple haze & now all I do is wait for Spring. Life is easier in your 40s.

ugly sweater
in lavender

ugly sweater
in brown & gray

ugly sweater
in royal blue

I am thoroughly sick of wearing sweaters every day, the very same sweaters that I was so excited to put on last Fall during these first invigorating cool days. Now that I've had them on for six months all my sweaters make me feel fat and ratty. Even the cashmere ones.

Winter lies too long in country towns, hangs on until it is shabby and old and sullen.
Willa Cather

Worn-out Winter
Worn-out Mittens

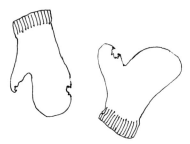

Winter wore out my mittens.

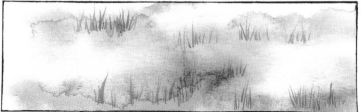

A beautiful kite blew into the Fox family's yard on Willowdale Avenue across from the Priory Lane last weekend. Given the wind direction, Annie Fox, who was gardening at the time, thinks that the kite must have come from the direction of Shore Park. If you have lost a kite, or know someone whose kite is lost, call her please.

44

Tea Cup Travel

Assam black tea tastes just as pungent and consoling in India as it does in Ireland. China green tea is complex and invigorating whether it's served in shot glasses in Tunisia or in a mug in Edinburgh. Darjeeling tastes the same in Africa as it does in Argentina, or in my kitchen on the Long Island Sound **where**:

I collect tea cups the way I used to collect days in foreign countries.

There's a tea cup, made of amber-colored glass, that's just like a shard of the Sahara glinting on my shelf.

The pale blue one — that's like a cup of Nottingham rain reflecting the face of a handsome stranger I was flirting with one afternoon 30 years ago.

Midnight blue Limoges is January in Paris, a rare snow fall in the city, cold kisses, and Jean-Claude.

My tea cup collection is my passport.

A TEA TIME MEMOIR   in Five Minuscule Chapters

1. Dublin

I was in the famous **Bewley's** tea room on Grafton Street. It was pouring rain. I glanced up from the letter I was writing to find that a young man my age (29? 30? — tweed jacket, tousled auburn hair, elegant hands) had invited himself to sit at my table. He had also invited himself to lean across his cup of tea and read the last paragraph of my letter to my sister Buffy. He met my indignant glare without a qualm. "You're left handed," he explained; "I thought you might be writing poetry."

Well I Never! I fled Bewley's in a fury. I wasn't used to being the object of a stranger's curiosity — but hadn't I traveled thousands of miles **JUST SO** I could be the kind of girl who writes poetry on rainy days in foreign countries? Now I was furious with myself. I swore that *no one* would *ever* catch me *not* writing poetry again.

2. London

Newly wed, in London solo. I want to live up to my **OLD SELF** in London, a city that always makes me feel glamorous, savvy, and free. I'm 32 and I hate all my clothes. At home I try to dress my age +"married" so I wear a lot of beige.

But I love this polka-dot top. For some reason I think that it is very hip and attention-getting. Wearing it feels like the good old days. London + polka-dots make me feel that I might be the kind of girl who has an affair! Runs away to France! Gets divorced!

At the Muffin Man in Kensington I'm trying to memorize the taste of tea in London ⌇ for my old self, for when I have to go back home to my beige clothes and husband.

3. Saint Malo

I'm here with the wrong man. This is my favorite town in France, an ancient stone walled village on the coast of Brittany. Narrow cobble-stone streets, well-lighted bistros, a tide that roars against the ramparts in thrilling sea — spraying waves. Here is the place for hours of unspoken communion with your soul mate.

But I'm here with the wrong man. Good Lord, he never shuts up. And his favorite (**only**) topic of conversation is **us** opinions and accusations and pleadings about **us**. Running away to France wasn't such a good idea after all.

I'm hiding out in this tea salon so I can figure out how to end this affair. I'm 34 and I know this for sure: The next time I come here it will be on my honeymoon with the Love of My Life. What I don't know is that I will have to wait until I am almost 50 years old for this to happen.

4. Buenos Aires

June, the first days of Winter. It is late afternoon and the café is nearly empty. The waiters are gathered at the bar, watching for customers and gossiping. I am 37 and in South America for the first time, collecting antiques and heirlooms for an auction house in New York. I have a new fiancé, a great job, plenty of money, and I'm pretty sure that this is the start of the rest of my untroubled life.

The Winter light is clear but pale. The window glass is the color of amber. The haze that fills the room is warm and soft, and there are a thousand harps playing Vivaldi in the background.   At least that's how I remember it. For years afterward, when all this has gone away – the fiancé, the job, the money – I will look back to this time and it will **glow**. For once, everything was golden.

5. Long Island Sound

It's my first cup of tea in the Village – black, with extra sugar, to go, from the Wolf's Lane Deli. It's also Moving Day! I've just dropped off my futon in the apartment next door and now I have to go sit on the park bench across the street and think about what I've got myself into.

   If this is going to be my permanent address, I better get some real furniture. That means a couch, and a coffee table, and ice cube trays. I've never owned ice cube trays; I don't own dinner plates, or dish towels, and I haven't started a CD collection. I don't own STUFF yet, and when I go shopping, I will discover that I am the kind of person who has opinions about shower curtains (nothing with flowers, or see-through).

   The Wolf's Lane Deli will be my best neighbor for the next 10 years. Barbara and John, the owners, will be kind to my cats and know all the news in advance of the weekly paper. The guys who work here, all good-looking and good-hearted, will hold mail for me, and spare keys and dry cleaning. Here is where I will buy many, many 10-pound bags of ice in the next decade because, sad to say, *not* buying ice cube trays will make me feel *wildly* undomesticated.

Wolf's Lane
DELI

2 ft. to 6 ft.
HEROS FOR ALL OCCASIONS

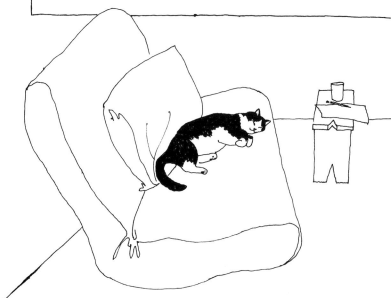

On the other side of the Village

Once in a while, for the ride into New York City, I treat myself to a **tea-to-go** from the kiosk at the train station. I stand on line behind the **regulars** who don't say a word. They lay down their dollar and the lady at the counter, having memorized so many faces, will have their *usual* ready in **seconds**, just in time for the 7:13 to Grand Central Terminal.

There are few hours in life more agreeable than the hour dedicated to the ceremony known as afternoon tea.

Henry James

IF YOU ARE COLD

Tea will warm you;
If you are too heated, it will cool you;
If you are depressed, it will cheer you;
If you are exhausted, it will calm you.

William Gladstone

Tea is Served in the

TEA... will always be the favored beverage of the intellectual...

THOMAS DE QUINCEY
Confessions of an English Opium-Eater

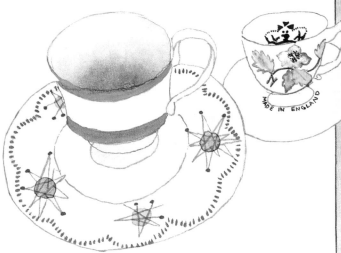

MADE IN ENGLAND

NOWHERE is the English genius for domesticity more notably evidenced than in the festival of afternoon tea.

G. Gissing

Temple of Longing

SOME DAYS "staying put" might feel the same as *Going Nowhere.*

Make a cup of tea and wait for that feeling to pass.

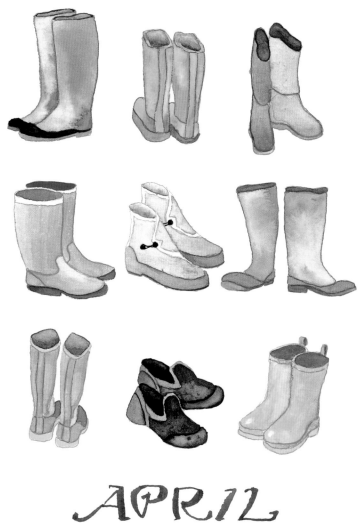

APRIL

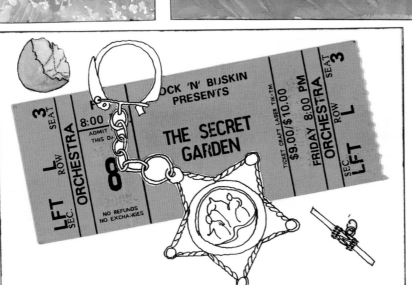

This is a chipmunk eating a
tulip petal.

APRIL is the LOST and FOUND MONTH

It's April and I can't wait to get out of the house! What with **Spring** shaking things up, people lose their grip on more than just Winter— and I collect it all, the lost key chains and watch fobs, the loose change and theater tickets that lay scattered on the streets of my Village this month, the **April Lost and Found**.

April is the month that sets the year in motion, **SHAKING** Winter loose, **TURNING** the world towards the sun, **BLOOMING** into nature's brightest colors. This change of season is so full of momentum **NO WONDER** we call it SPRING.

Lost and Found on the Road
from SLIGO to ZINDERNEUF

When I was a *traveler* every day was April

◊ In Galway I stood in the rain for *five hours* trying to hitch a ride **east** to Dublin. But I found a new direction the instant someone stopped and offered me a ride up **north**: "Can I take you to Yeats country?" was all he had to ask.

◊ In the midst of a road trip thru England I took off and lost myself in Africa for two weeks. **TUNISIA**. I'd never even *heard* of the place until I saw a poster of the warm and sunny ruins of **Carthage** in a travel agency window on Tavern Street in Ipswich. The **cold rain** pouring down on my head was all it took to inspire in me a sudden and profound interest in Roman ruins in the north Sahara, on the Mediterranean coast.

◊ The rainy season washes out the only road in the southern Sahara between Timbuktu and Cotonou. You never know who you'll find among the stranded travelers. One year I found a Fulbright scholar who asked me to teach him embroidery and we sewed a Celtic alphabet together. The next year I found a Zen Buddhist from Louisiana who was the best kisser I ever met in the 1980s.

Staying Put
didn't put an end to my road trips. Not when there was 25 ¼ miles of roads within the town limits. I had a map that I'd torn out of the Village telephone book, so I knew where to go. I figured I could walk each and every street in a month or two... maybe it would take all Spring *at the most*.

It took seven years.
I walked every street, over and over. I walked year round. I walked in snow storms and I walked in heat waves. I walked from east to west, and then I walked west to east. I walked on the sunny side of the street, and then I crossed the road and walked on the shady side. I back-tracked and side-tracked, I took short cuts and I went back around the long way. I walked until I could draw my own map ∼ of every waterfall, stone wall, sundial and cemetery. I walked so I could draw it all by heart.

America's great philosopher of Staying Put, Henry David Thoreau, bragged that he was not a traveler "except for being well traveled in Concord [his hometown]." He said: "My vicinity affords many good walks. Two or three hours' walking will carry me to as strange a country as I expect ever to see. A single farmhouse which I had not seen before is sometimes as good as the dominions of the King of Dahomey."

April 1

WOW! Daylight Savings Time is in effect and suddenly the afternoon seems endless - so much light! It was warm, too, so I took a long walk to the farthest street in the Village, and on Maple Ave. I found a penny with a heart-shaped hole in it.

April 4

The tulips are in bloom, but I don't think that this warm spell is here to stay. It never is, in April.

April 7

Freezing temperatures again. Then, at sunset: *Snow.* This is why we don't put away our Winter coats until *May.*

April 8

Rain today - it washed away all the snow.

April 10

In the woods there was a single pink tulip in bloom, between the roots of an ancient beech tree, in plain sight by the south end of the main street through town. So it was a wonder that the beautiful flower stood there for three whole days before someone picked it today.

April 14

Hundreds of buttercups are blooming in the meadow near the high school. They were not there yesterday and now they're everywhere!

April 15

The only café in the Village put tables out on the sidewalk today. This begins our Outdoor Dining Season. These three tables will be the center of our café society from now until the first frost.

April 18

It isn't unusual, in our Village Library, to find mementos left behind in library books: a list of things to remember, a valentine, a confession. Today I found a photograph of a boy (tucked into a book of local history), on a by-gone Summer day, sitting with his arms around his baseball bat. (He looks unhappy.) One day, I hope I'll find a love letter.

April 20

I wish my old cat, Woody Robinson, were here to see the wild violets in bloom today. When he was old and blind I used to carry him across the road so he could sit in the sun and sniff his favorite flowers. Now when I see these violets bloom every year they don't look right without an old black & white cat tucked up in their midst, asleep, purring in the sun.

April 21

Rain all day.

April 25

Heavy rain, then just a drizzle with a mist. Then: a drippity, drenching downpour. Almost every kind of April rain.

April 27

My Village is 6,000 miles from the Amazon, yet today I found a parrot feather, of all things, right on the sidewalk. A huge turquoise and yellow parrot feather! I brought it home to show the cats and they couldn't believe it either!

April 30

I found a kroner on the sidewalk today. An *Iceland* kroner coin from the little island nation in the middle of the North Atlantic Ocean, 3,000 miles from here. It's only worth ⅓ of an American penny but to me it's another *treasure* for my April Lost and Found.

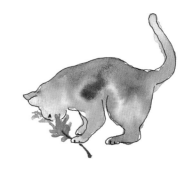

Our April 7 snowstorm cancelled school, the weekly senior citizens meeting and the Yankees' opening day home baseball game. Blooming daffodils lost their blossoms but, luckily, many had not yet bloomed.

1776
OLDEST HOUSE in VILLAGE
HOME OF
COLONEL DAVID PELL
AMERICAN PATRIOT

Rain Book

Rainy days on the Long Island Sound ~
a good reason for Staying Put

pouring   drenching   drizzle   spritz

driving   dripping   soaking   mist

Rainy season, West
Africa. No raincoats or
umbrellas for us Peace
Corps Volunteers.
Only one kind of rain:
   DELUGE.
 22 inches of rain in two
months. And it's 90°~
walking in the rain
was *fun*.

April on the Long Island
Sound: it's not Africa.

But *this* is fun ~
my vintage raincoat, a
harlequin-patterned vinyl
slicker with corduroy
collar and cuffs ($8.00
at the local thrift shop).

History in the Mist · The Company of Peacocks · August by the Fireside
It's the rainy days I remember best
A RAINY DAYS MEMOIR in Three Minuscule Chapters

1. ENGLAND

The ancestral homeland. In 1976 it's still possible to be the first American some English people have ever met. I'm 20, and I've never met a **real horse**, like here in Leicestershire in a village called Copt Oak. Amusements consist of a red phone box, a bus stop, and a church. I have no one to call and no bus to catch so I walk to the churchyard to look for the tree ~ the Copt Oak ~ that's been here for 2,500 years. It's so quiet, I could have heard myself pray. Instead, I listen to these horses, sighing and shaking rain out of their manes, the same way that horses have stood in the rain here for 2,500 years.

2. JORDAN VALLEY

September Peacocks like cat food. I throw pellets to them when they stroll thru the yard every afernoon.
October The peacocks are molting. I gather their tail feathers and put them in a vase. These days they tap their beaks on my door for the crackers that they eat out of my hand.
November At the start of the Winter rains I invite the peacocks to come inside. And with the most exquisite manners I've ever seen in birds, they keep me quiet company while I make their hot buttered toast.

3. DONEGAL BAY

Donegal Bay is a hot spot for European surfers. Being from America, I equate surfing with California sunshine and the happy-go-lucky hipster dudes of my homeland, not the Old World drizzle of the Connaught coast and the dismal, self-conscious Euro-teens of my experience (who, *in my experience,* all seem to be **big** Leonard Cohen fans – need I say more?).

    I'm sitting here, in the mist in a graveyard on a shore at the edge of Western civ-ilization, trying to meditate on my up-coming 30th birthday. I consider this a significant event in the 4-billion-year history of the Earth. Today is a significantly dreary day, cold, with significantly dark rain clouds, consequently there are no surfers about. I try to think significant thoughts, but instead I keep snickering at the thought of Liechtensteinians hanging ten. So I just eat the picnic lunch I bought at a cafeteria in town (a hard boiled egg sandwich with yellowman toffee for dessert).

    Oh well. It's tea time now, and I walk back into town. There's a pub here that, even though it's August, keeps a fire roaring in the public bar to ward off the perpetual damp. I order a cup of tea and I huddle close to the hearth.

    Then Seóise arrives, with rain in his hair and my invitation to the ceili.

    He was right; the craic, it was good.

    I love rainy days that turn into dancing all night.

William Lightbody, 80

William Lightbody, a resident of the Village for 75 years, has died at the age of 80. He graduated from the High School, where he was captain of the football team. He served in the Army in World War II, attaining rank of Sergeant, in Burma, India, and China. He will be remembered for his famous walks down Main Street, hand in hand with his wife Dorothy and at least one dog on a leash.

HENRY DAVID THOREAU, PHILOSOPHER of THE WALK:

I HAVE MET WITH BUT ONE or TWO PERSONS in the course of my life who understood the art of WALKING, that is, of taking walks — who had a genius, so to speak, for SAUNTERING.

There is in fact a sort of harmony discoverable between the landscape within...the limits of an afternoon walk, and the threescore years and ten of human life.

It requires a direct dispensation from Heaven to become a walker. You must be born into the family of walkers.

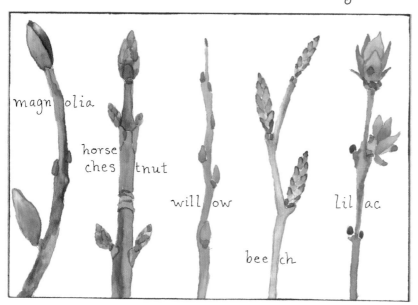

magnolia

horse chestnut

willow

beech

lilac

AMBULATOR NASCITUR NON FIT

WALKERS ARE BORN, NOT MADE

Elvira Jeanette Parmesean, 81

Elvira Jeanette Parmesean has died at the age of 81. She lived in the Village for 48 years. Known as "Elvira", "Vera", "Jeannie", or "Jean", her family said, "Her friends will miss her wit, bright spirit and humor, and her family will miss her guidance and direction. She loved her daily walks on the shore road."

A WALKER'S LOST & FOUND

$16.74 ⅓. One year I saved all the loose change I found on the sidewalk. Then I spent it on toys for the cats at the local animal shelter.

Three golden pillowy pancakes on the side of the street across from the library, in a row ～ *waiting for a lift?*

On another road, a perfectly intact package of 8 hamburger buns, flattened by traffic, flatter than pancakes.

In the creek on the edge of town, an entire set of dishes - plates, cups, saucers — flung into the mud, sinking under a foot of water. Imagine the strange mix of fury and determination it takes to **do** that, to ignore that little voice in your head that pleads, as you storm out of the house with your arms full of crockery the whole time you march towards the creek, *Whoa! This is a <u>total</u> waste of dinnerware!*

A **drawbridge** on the far border of the Village, over the old Barge Canal. At the controls in the Bridge House for 30 years is Robert Borzacchini, who considers this drawbridge and this canal to be his Walden, and I have an open invitation whenever I walk by to stop in and discuss the weather, the winds, the secret language of trees.

Hello Kaboodle!

ving **COUPON**
e Sea **TUNA**
29¢
(Limit 2)

ALVERNIA HIGH SCHOOL SENIOR CLASS '68

**Sunday
April 21**

Curtain
8:00 p.m.

PRESENTS
DAVID AND LISA
ALVERNIA AUDITORIUM
3901 North Ridgeway Avenue
Admission $2.00

RESERVED SEAT
Section L
Row B
Seat 3

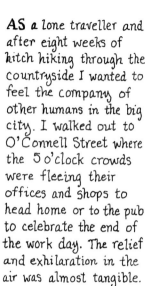

DUBLIN

AS a lone traveller and after eight weeks of hitch hiking through the countryside I wanted to feel the company of other humans in the big city. I walked out to O'Connell Street where the 5 o'clock crowds were fleeing their offices and shops to head home or to the pub to celebrate the end of the work day. The relief and exhilaration in the air was almost tangible.

LOSS AVERSION

is what we call the in-born knowledge that the pain of LOSS lasts longer than the pleasure of GAIN. The pleasure of GETTING is fleeting; the pain of LOSING can last a lifetime. So people will avoid any situation where there is even a *slight* chance of loss ⟶ not just loss of **stuff** but even loss of what is **familiar**, no matter how boring or bad the **familiar** is.
LOSS AVERSION is why most people have a strong preference for the status quo.

Some losses last longer than a lifetime. In my Village the ghost of Widow Parrish haunts her **OLD STONE HOUSE** for the gold coins that she buried there over 150 years ago. During her life she was much vexed for having forgotten the hiding place that kept her fortune safe from robbers, so she is still roaming the property, looking for her lost treasure.

After an hour's walk I was tired, and cold. I found a genial pub, went inside, and ordered a well-earned sherry. Pulling off my gloves and patting down my hair, I discovered that I was missing an earring. I'd lost it on the streets of Dublin.

Now, about that earring: It was Indian, purchased six months before in Washington, D.C. I'd gone there with my new boyfriend, a semi-famous composer who was conducting two performances of the Juilliard Orchestra at the Kennedy Center. I was *quite* dazzled with myself in D.C. **This** was how I imagined it would be, my glamorous new life as the much younger wife of a DISTINGUISHED MUSICIAN, hopping on jets every weekend, a pampered V.I.P. at famous concert halls.

But soon after we checked into the Watergate Hotel, the DISTINGUISHED MUSICIAN let it slip that he was already married. (There was a little dog in the lobby and he said, "We have one of those at home." I said, "**WE?!**") I stormed out of the hotel to blow off steam, the DISTINGUISHED MUSICIAN slinking after me. "I thought you knew!" he had the nerve to say, as if he were **SO** famous that I would have read about him in People magazine.

I paused at a shop window to admire some earrings, the very earrings I've brought here to Dublin with me when I decided that I had to get a new life away from lying, cheating married men. Of course the DISTINGUISHED MUSICIAN insisted on buying them for me, to show what a great guy he was.

This is how much I *hate* to lose anything: after all these years I've completely forgotten the DISTINGUISHED MUSICIAN's name, or how I had the pleasure of dumping him. But I remember **Every thing** – the names of back streets near the River Liffey, the handsome face of a young man wearing a cape on Grafton Street, how I wondered *could I marry a guy who wears a cape?*, the way the sweet sherry warmed my heart on a cold Summer evening – **Everything** about losing that earring.

Woody's violets on Wolf's Lane

If there is just one thing I want you to know about **APRIL** it's that

Everyone has lost
               Something Precious.

That's why people are so cranky. So go easy on one another.
               We're all here to help each other find whatever we've lost.

PRECIOUS FRIEND
Woody Robinson
1980 - 1996

MAY

There's a strange new sound everywhere, a roar of murmurs. It's the May breeze rustling in the trees, the leaves making the sh-sh-shushhhhhhing sound of a thousand secrets.

From November to April the trees are silent. Not a sound, day or night. But now every branch is full of leaves and the trees are suddenly full of echos. The noise spreads from tree to tree with every gust of wind, like a conversation of urgent whispers.

I Love Secrets
And here come 31 days of them!
Of course I'm staying put in May.

MAY is the Month of Secrets

I found *three* cards in the grass on the Village Green — playing cards:

3 of Spades
8 of Diamonds
3 of Hearts

I'm *sure* it *must* be a secret message.
But what can it mean?

Here's a clue:
1. **Spades** = SWORDS
2. **DIAMONDS** are Pentacles
3. **Hearts** MEAN **CUPS**

The Secret to Staying Put:
CULTIVATE A SECRET GARDEN

My elderly neighbor is building a stone wall. It all started when he widened his driveway a few months ago. This caused a ruckus at the Village Supervisor's office because the new driveway was six inches wider than the building codes allowed. There were Town Meetings, and more Town Meetings, about whether or not the new driveway had to be re-done, to be like the **old** driveway. Almost everybody in the Village had an opinion about it, and plenty of nasty accusations and counter-accusations were made by supporters of the new driveway and backers of the old one.

In the end, the old man was allowed to keep his driveway but he was bitter. So, to keep Village busy-bodies from ever nosing into his business again, the old man is building a stone wall around his property. (Strange that there doesn't seem to be a code against building a big spiteful stone wall.)

If you came to my Village and you saw this big stone wall going up at the end of my street, you might think that there must be something **wonderful** behind it. Perhaps a secret garden where rare orchids thrive, or a diving pool inlaid with Persian turquoise, or an aviary filled with ivory-billed woodpeckers. You would never guess that all that secrecy behind the stone wall was for a ***driveway***. Different people put different things in their secret gardens, is all I'm saying.

May 1

The landscape that I know so well when it's laid bare in Winter is unrecognizable in May. It is impossible to see anything familiar through so much greenery. No more open spaces, only enclosures and hidden views. What's the big secret being kept behind those thick hedges and deep within those boughs?

May is more mysterious than most people think.

May 4

It took 123 days to happen but here it is: the first *perfect* day of the year!

The air is like wine - a delicate white wine, perhaps Vouvray, drunk on the banks of the Loire.

Barbara Pym, from *A Glass of Blessings*

May 5

I discovered a fine patch of white violets growing in the park across the street. If secrets could be flowers, they'd be white violets.

May 6

I wait all year for this day, when the cherry trees are in bloom and I make myself dizzy under their boughs, as if I am afloat in a cascade of pink cherry blossom froth.

May 10

It's the first time this year that I'm in the garden after dark. It's midnight and the air is still warm. Trees, full of leaves with nothing to do, catch the moonlight, scatter it in bright shadows here and there. And, in the dark, a new sound, moving from tree to tree: new leaves rustling in the breeze ～ I imagine that I hear waves, applause, conversations half-heard. May is the month of secrets, whispered everywhere.

May 13

The cherry blossoms are falling apart, dropping in the millions, cherry blossom petals everywhere, a lather of pink flowers floating in the breeze, drifting like surreal snowflakes.

May 16

I watched an elderly neighbor build a stone wall today. He took all the time in the world picking a rock from the jumble of boulders heaped on the ground, setting it on top of one already in the wall, sipping his brandy, pondering the next rock. Brandy seems to be a very important part of the stone wall building process.

May 23

It was so cold today that I made oatmeal for breakfast, like I do in Winter. I drank my afternoon tea in bed, wrapped up in my blankets. Phooey.

May 25

I needed to buy cat food for my five cats, which I get in big 20-lb. bags that I drag home in my shopping trolly. So I walked down the road and the man who owns the Antiques Shop saw me with my silly trolly and he smiled: "Aha!" he said. "It must be cat food day!" I have no secrets. Have I?

May 31

Warm again! Such a beautiful day, nothing bad could happen on a day like this. I put on my pretty pink Spring jacket and I walked to the woods on the south side of the Village ～ and discovered that *it was gone!* Vanished, chopped down to make way for a parking garage. My heart broke.

Good thing there was an angel there, whispering to me, telling me how hearts can heal. No kidding. An *angel*. Spoke to *me*.

Garden Notes

Visitors to our homes form their first impressions at the curb. Just ask any real estate agent. A warm and welcoming entry can be created by landscaping, softening the hard edges of steps and stoops, the harsh textures of stone, brick, and concrete walkways. Low shrubs planted near the front façade are standard, but the inclusion of color in the form of flowers adds just that extra softness and warmth. Throughout the Village there are numerous warmly welcoming front walks and enticing entrances.

HOW TO BUILD A STONE WALL

1. Use Native Stones ~ local stones fit into the landscape better

2. Old walls are the best source of stone. If an old wall has fallen apart it's no longer a wall and it's fair to pick out good stones *but* it's a sin to pick apart an intact wall.

3. A stone wall is really 2 walls, front and back, that lean into each other (the lean is called the *batter*). The walls should lean inward ½ inch per 1 ft. of height.

4. Put the oddest-looking stones on the bottom.

5. If you have a really pretty rock, try to find a place for it on the top or edge of the wall.

The weight of stone = water

62 pounds per cubic foot.

Cognac mixed with water is called *fine a l'eau* and was very popular before WWII or so I'm told.
Serve in a pony glass.
Stone wall optional.

left
A white picket fence on Wolf's Lane.

White roses, lavender, and silver-leaf Artemisia. This garden is the flower form of twilight.

The Church of Shepherd and Bloom

Shepherd and Bloom were planted in the 1970s on the shore of Glenwood Lake. They've grown to be **enormous**, the biggest cherry trees you've ever seen. The two trees lean into one another, their branches knitting together overhead into a single high dome. When their boughs are full of cherry blossoms you can enter this space and it feels sacred, soft, and safe, in every direction, forever.

The Snowflake Gardener is what I called this neighbor ⌒ He glued silver plastic snowflakes on the leaves of his hosta plants, "To add a little sparkle," he told me.
The snowflakes glowed in the dark.

Secret Gardens and other Out of the Way Places

The Old Stone House (haunted) **Garden**
Gone now, sold off and cleared for construction of another (second) house squeezed onto the property.

above
Secret entrances into the woods

right
The Herb Garden at the Founder's Manor, home to descendants of the first Lord of the Manor. The house was destroyed in the American Revolution and rebuilt in 1842. Hardly anyone comes to this far corner of the old manorplace.

The Secret Garden
that *every other* SECRET GARDEN will be compared to

The Geffrye Museum isn't on most tourist maps of London. It's tucked away in the East End, in an area called **Shoreditch** named for an ancient "sewer ditch" from when this was the boggy end of town. For almost 100 years the museum has exhibited its vast collection of home furnishings depicting five centuries of the English Domestic Interior, arranged in room settings in chronological order in buildings that were once the poor houses of the Ironmonger's Company.

"It is a fascinating place," wrote one English lady shortly after the museum opened during WWI, "like a rather badly arranged old curiosity shop."

There's an herb garden hidden behind the museum. There are 170 different herbs planted here: **cosmetic culinary medicinal household aromatic**

Most people don't know this: The best way to visit an herb garden is **in the rain**. Rain drops plop on the plants and **boing!** the air is full of the scent of sage and lavender. Plus, in the rain, you will probably have the garden **all to yourself.**

Come in from the rain to the tea room at the Geffrye, which offers light refreshments (*savory cabbage rolls, sandwiches with choice of filling, cake*) and English wine by the glass or bottle. *English wine!*

To Soothe
To Savor
To Anoint
To Refresh

1.

2.

THANK GOD
THEY CANNOT
CUT DOWN
THE
CLOUDS

Henry David Thoreau,
Walking 1857

3.

Neglected. Overgrown. Wild. *Wonderful.*

There aren't many secret corners in my Village. Inhabited since 1654, there isn't much land in my Village that hasn't been claimed & settled, surveyed, ploughed, cleared, mowed, or fenced in. So when I found a little Eden in a vacant lot on the edge of town I kept it to myself. Flourishing in the neglect, among the weeds and scrubrush, was the most magnificent mulberry bush anyone has ever seen ⟶ or, that NO ONE but ME has ever seen. It was my favorite secret garden of all.

1.

III of SWORDS

Absence
Disappointment
Removal
Delay

2.

Expertise
Artistic
Ability

Dignity
Crafts-
manship

VIII of PENTACLES

3.

III of CUPS

Conclusion
Resolution
Solace
Healing
Fulfillment

In Summer I came here for the best shade in town. To enter the dark leafy cave of this mulberry bush I had to kneel under branches drooping from the weight of fat, juicy, ripe black berries. If I dared to **breathe** on a leaf, berries would shower down on me, warm squishy splatters of soft berry rain. I don't know how many times this made me laugh *but it always made me laugh.*

It's gone now. The last lot of wilderness, with my mulberry refuge, all gone. Chopped down, scraped clean to make room for — what else? — a parking garage.

Just when my heart broke I heard the voice of an angel. So kind and gentle (I never talk to *myself* that way, so it *had* to be the voice of an angel), the voice said: YOU WILL GET BACK WHAT YOU'VE LOST.

Angels are so easy to understand. Or maybe it's the secrets of life that are so easy to understand. Like the one about how life is about losing and finding another mulberry bush, or something else just as sweet, sheltering, and real.

And another thing, whispering from the memory of my mulberry bush: **LET GO**.

Hearing is believing. It doesn't matter if its the sound of an angel or a breeze in a mulberry bush.

Eden is that old-fashioned **House**
We dwell in every day
Without suspecting our abode
Until we drive away

How fair on looking back, the **Day**
We sauntered from the Door--
Unconscious our returning,
But discover it no more.

Emily Dickinson (1830-1886)

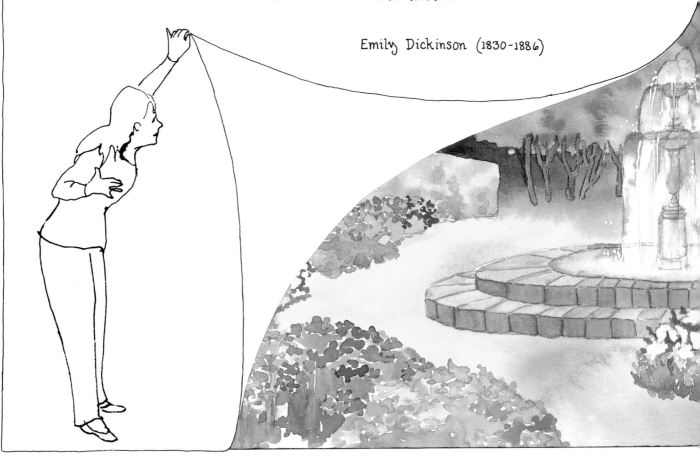

Seeds for a Secret Garden

June

Previous page:

The majority of Earth's inhabitants (4-6 million species) HAVE WINGS.
To an insect AIR is as thick as HONEY.

I collect Blue Jay feathers. I have 2. One day, I hope I'll find a 3rd.

It's **June** and anything can happen!
Of course, it usually *doesn't*... but still...

Now that I'm grown up I don't get to make very many interesting decisions about myself anymore.

It didn't use to be this way. I remember what it used to be like, in my traveling days, when there was so much to figure out about myself that I changed my mind every other day! And overhauled the possibilities drastically!

I might go kick up my heels in Paris and be a **Vivienne!** (They called me Vivi for short.)

I could traipse through Merlin's enchanted Celtic forest and turn into **Vyvyan!** (Almost pulled it off in the Summer of '76.)

I could be a pioneer on an avocado farm in the Galilee and call myself **Aviva!** (I seriously thought I could do this. I lasted one week.)

But these days it's more likely that I'll be making a decision about new curtains than a new alias.

So: it's June's job to remind me that there are still surprises in the air, glittering like dragonflies' wings. Because June is *full* of marvelous winged things, butterflies, blue jays, bemusements, and bumblebees, fluttering everywhere. That sparkle in the air? It might be my next change of mind. That weightless sense of flight? It could be me, winging to a new adventure. Anything can happen. *It's June.*

JUNE is the
Month With Wings

I've seen all kinds of Junes.

In Alaska I saw the midnight sun hover over an arctic Summer June, in Buenos Aires I saw a mid-afternoon night fall in a Winter June. I know what June is like, under layers of wool sweaters in the Scottish Highlands, and what it's like, *wishing* I had layers of *something* on the nude beaches on the Côte d'Azur. Also, Saharan Junes, Sierra Junes, Roman ruin Junes, and Rio de Janeiro Junes. **And now: A June with feathers.**

I watched crows playing in the spray of a water sprinkler on the lawn in front of the Village Gazebo. The birds chased each other through the waterfall, and then took turns posing in the mist, drenching their feathers and showing off their fearlessness. I swear I heard them laugh.

Crow's play.
We have a lot to learn from crows.

June 1
So. Last month I heard an angel. Nothing surprises me any more. And that's the problem – it's been so long since I've been astonished that I've gotten out of the habit. It's no fun being blasé but at a certain age, it's inevitable. And then it's June and I'm amazed every day.

June 3
It's so HOT. The heat makes me notice how heavy the air is, thick, weighty – so *this* is how it feels to be a butterfly!

June 5
Shade! In June I need shade for the first time all year. What a difference it makes, to walk into shadows where the air is cooler, of course, but also denser, sweeter; like the air in dreams.

June 8
Rain today, just a mist sweet with the scent of honeysuckle and dust. It wasn't really a *real* rain, it was a Juney kind of rain, hardly there at all.

June 10
I was taking my Winter coat to the dry cleaner's – all I had on my mind was errands and ennui – and I found a blue jay feather on the sidewalk! Shed, no doubt, from the wing of my gaudy guardian angel.

June 14
A little brown bird, flying with a very long pink ribbon in her beak, landed on the sidewalk in front of me to rest. I watched her catch her breath and launch herself up in the air again, the ribbon flowing in the air behind her, her signature in the wind.

June 16
In this heat I would be happy to wear nothing but my African sarongs all day long, like when I lived on the Sahara. Now, I would never go out in *public* wearing one, even though it was acceptable street wear in Moslem West Africa. Because, alas, Africa is 3,000 miles ~ and 20 years ~ away from me now.

June 20
A woman in the next town has a dragonfly sanctuary in her backyard and every now and then a flock of the ones called *skimmers* drifts into the Village. I saw dragonflies floating down Main Street this afternoon, like a cloud of golden glitter in the air.

June 22
Rain today. The cats and I watched it come down, pool into a great wash of rainwater in the street. At twilight, it glowed with the colors of the setting sun and the street lamp. A Juney puddle of rain, full of light.

June 26
Hot again today, *African* hot. I walked past a stone wall at dusk and I felt the residual heat glowing off the rocks. I touched the wall, felt the warmth of billion-year-old cosmic light, as if the stones had a memory of when they were stardust.

June 30
I dragged my kitchen stool out to Main Street to check out the bird's nest in the awning above the Village's dive bar. I peered in, and 3 bug-eyed babies stared back! They were surrounded by dive-bar nesting materials: shredded cigarette filters, cellophane, tin foil from trash on the sidewalk. And one pink ribbon.

Lawn Ornament "Returns" After Absence of Two Years

Recently, this lawn ornament appeared in front of the home of Phyllis Lane. It had been stolen two years ago. A hand printed note tied to the little man said: "Dear Lady of the House, Please excuse my absence. I've traveled far and wide and I've told all I've met of you and your great love that you show all of your lawn ornaments. I missed my home and I hope you will accept me and care for me as you always have.
With Love & Sincerity, G-Nome."

JUNE reminds me of something
I FORGET every Winter ∿
Shade is different from
Regular Air

SHADE falls from trees Heavy ∿
full of shadows from so many yesterdays

A QUIET hiding place for long-lost
midnight breezes

Shade is where you go
to think the thoughts
that come from cooler, dimmer shores

ANOTHER HOT DAY

And when the sun goes down
relief from the
searing heat
comes from the ground up.

EVERY BLADE of GRASS
cools off **one by one**

and when I walk into the meadow at
the end of the day I can feel the

TWILIGHT
on my ankles.

In my 20s I was a situational nudist, as in *trying not to look mortified on a topless beach in the South of France* kind of situational nudist.

When I came to live in Africa I dicovered how *relaxing* modesty was.

Niger is one of the hottest countries on Earth, and the Muslim ladies there don't parade around in their all-over tans. They wear the *pagne*, a sarong-style garment, a yard-long piece of cloth that you wrap around your body and secure in place by rolling the top edge inside-out. Wrapped up all the way to their ankles, the African women moved like mermaids.

Me, I wore the *pagne* as a mini-dress. And I discovered how much better it was to be covered up, because, unlike being naked, you don't have to hold in your stomach.

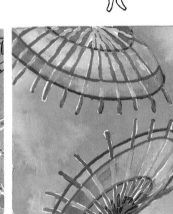

African fabric, collected by me in the Republic of Niger, 1980-1982

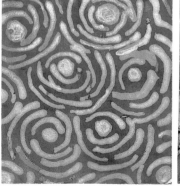

silk skirt

rayon skirt

7 sleeveless tops with various necklines

cool zipper-y vest

SIX of these cotton turtle-necks

heavy-knit turtle-neck

cotton sweater

wool knit with mother-of-pearl buttons

Long-sleeved T

lacey vest

ankle length vest — never worn YET but one day I'll need to

2 not-so-low-cut V-necks

low-cut V-neck

silky palazzo pants

boot-cut dressy trousers

favorite black jeans

94

LADY-LIKE BLACK
Tailored wool crepe with *covered* buttons

IRONIC BLACK
You don't think I take take these jewel-tone buttons *seriously*, do you?

BLACK VELVET BLACK
Velvet collar and buttons hint that this jacket knows a thing or two about decadence.

SIX SHADES of BLACK

I came, I **stayed put,** I ended up with a closet full of the wrong clothes. Now I have nothing to wear, **NOTHING** in the right shade of **BLACK** for a fine **JUNE** day.

POWER TRIP BLACK
Wrap-around wool with a bit of a cape to throw over my shoulder, for making a grand entrance.

DOWNTOWN BLACK
So Minimalist. So avant-garde

IN HEAVEN EVERYONE IS 30. THIS IS WHAT I'LL BE WEARING IN THE AFTER LIFE BLACK
Metal studs and zippers all over myself. I turned 30 in the 1980s and I still think this look is FABULOUS.

An African Memoir

in Four Minuscule Chapters

1. Morning in the Sahara

I was a brand new Peace Corps Volunteer, exulting in my status as one of Life's Adventurers. I sat on my balcony and surveyed my domain: a one-room flat in a "dormitory" of foreign workers, starting tomorrow, a job at the National Museum; a paycheck of $70.00 every month; a plastic lawn chair on a balcony with a view of a narrow sandy yard with a few scraggly shade trees. I sipped my tea and sighed. Life was good.

A movement in the branches caught my eye. It was a little brown monkey, clambering through the tree tops. I barely paid attention to it. "This is *Africa*," I told myself, world-wearily. "There are going to be monkeys *everywhere*."

If only I had bothered to read a single thing about Africa to prepare for this great adventure, I would have known that in the Sahara *there are no monkeys*. For two years I sat on that balcony, drinking my morning tea, never seeing another monkey in my yard, wishing for something *interesting* to happen.

3. Night in Tunisia

Jasmine and frankincense from perfume merchants in the souk. Peacocks in the labyrinthine gardens, pecking into the flower beds for scarabs. Paul Klee discovered color here in Carthage (his art was never the same). The sun goes down, oil lamps are lit in the minarets. The only sound is the sea & the cooling breeze on the desert sand. I'm 20, and this here is the dividing line between who I *was* and who I *will be*.

2. High Noon

They say it's the oldest life form in Africa, and the longest living. The mighty Baobab tree gives a thousand years of shade, shelter, and food to the more ephemeral creatures of the savannah ... such as us humans.

A large bull in the herd of elephants we'd been tracking since dawn turned and flapped his ears at us. It was a warning: Don't come any closer. My friend the wildlife biologist coasted our jeep to the nearest Baobab tree, using its wide trunk to hide us in plain sight.

We hadn't noticed the napping baboons. Baobab fruit is a baboon's favorite food, and we'd blundered into the middle of a baboon picnic party, disturbing their siesta. One by one the baboons roused themselves to stare at us. One barked, a few yawned, all showing their fearsome pointed teeth. People here consider a baboon to be as dangerous as a *panther*; here were **thirty** of them. And they were waking up *fast*. In the other direction there was an annoyed elephant sniffing the air for our scent.

I've never been so NOT bored.

4. Lawn Party at the American Embassy

It's blazing hot and the conversation is suffocating : raising children, their boarding schools, the cost of living. It was my first important lesson in international bores.

I wandered away from what was technically U.S. territory to the edge of the property where, at the bottom of the Ambassador's cliff, the *real* Africa began. There flowed the Niger River, which the nomads of West Africa call "the river of rivers". On its banks, men and women beat their laundry against rocks. On its broad, still surface, fishermen steered their canoes upriver, in the direction of Timbuktu. The river and the shimmering sky were the same dusty gold color.

POW

Something snapped, exploded, split the air right in front of me. Something . . . *turquoise?*

"What was *that?!*" I asked, spinning around to face the handsome man who had followed me to the frontier. A wildlife biologist, I found out later, here to study elephants.

"That was an Abyssinian Roller," he said. My mind went blank. "It's a *bird*," he explained, smiling. He was my first important lesson in wildlife biologists.

I've dreamt of Africa for three decades now, and in my dreams I'm always flying ～ over the velvet green hills of Zanzibar or the glittering pink sands of Mali. Sometimes I swoop low into the shade of the Cameroon forest, sometimes I soar so high that I touch the peak of Kilimanjaro.

MY HEART is like A BIRD

BRILLIANT · Breathtaking Daring

The Abyssinian Roller is one of 12 Old World birds, all called Rollers, named for the dives and somersaults they perform in flight. The Abyssinian Roller is widely distributed in the savannah of the southern Sahara. They are sturdy birds, resembling jays, and are a vivid blue with long tail streamers. They are pugnacious and noisy and fearless, and will dive at humans and other intruders.

O YOU BEAUTIFUL BIRDS ～ FLY WITH ME ANY TIME

Sassy · Noisy · BRAVE

The Blue Jay is one of the most attractive birds in North America. The jay prefers woods but visits gardens close to the forest, and does not migrate in Winter; is able to mimic the voices of other birds and various other sounds but usually scolds and shrieks in nasal screams or flutelike calls. The Blue Jay is not shy and gives a piece of its mind to owls & hawks, teases cats, and scares snakes.

In 1787 the famous English traveler William Beckford visited the ESCURIAL MONASTERY in Spain, where he was shown a **feather** from the **wing** of the **Archangel Gabriel**. He said: *It was displayed lying stretched out upon a quilted silken mattress, the most glorious specimen of plumage ever beheld in terrestrial regions, full three feet long, and of a blushing hue more soft and delicate than that of the loveliest rose.*

Satyrid Family
straight line, fluttering
up and down

Nymphalid Family
straight line with long,
low loops

Pierid Family
low, looping
zig-zag

IN GREECE
IF you see a white moth in your house do not DISTURB it.
It is only a VISITING ANCESTOR or some other DEPARTED SOUL.
IT WILL NOT HARM YOU.

A BUTTERFLY FLAPS HER WINGS IN THE AMAZON
AND CREATES a RAINBOW in ANTARCTICA.

PETALOUDIA meaning OPEN PETAL is *Modern Greek*
for BUTTERFLY. *In Ancient Greek* the word was PSYCHE.

In **Madagascar** some people believe
they are descended *from* BUTTERFLIES.

MAYANS venerated DRAGONFLIES
as the spirit of QUETZALCOATL, the mighty
feathered serpent SKY GOD. In INDIA
they believe that after the death of a PERSON
the soul is TRANSFORMED into a DRAGONFLY
while it awaits REINCARNATION.

July

Summer
Mind

Champagne at Midnight

Champagne at Noon

My desire for knowledge is intermittent, but my desire to bathe my head in atmospheres unknown to my feet is perennial and constant.

Henry David Thoreau
Walking, 1862

In 1688 Dom Perignon, a blind monk in France, discovered *champagne*. He cried out to his fellow clerics: "Brothers! Come quick! I have tasted the stars!"

Ah
The NIGHT LIFE
is why I stay put in July.

JULY is the PARTY of the YEAR

There's no better time than NOW to
dress up and dance all night ~
to celebrate the wildest longings of
your SUMMER MIND.
Nothing is too extreme to come true,
Nothing is impossible for July ~
My heart is SKY HIGH.

Some nights
it's too hot to sleep.

So I push my pillow to
the far end of my mattress and
I lay my head in the direction
of the South Pole. Now that
my toes are in the Northern
Hemisphere of my bed, soaking
in all that nervous energy, my
mind is experiencing the effects
of the Southern Hemisphere.

It's Winter there, and
my over-excited brain is in a
cold front near Tierra del
Fuego. The pressure drops. There
is frost in the air. Snow begins
to fall. The atmosphere becomes
sweet with silence. Except for
the sound of icy waves breaking
against a frozen shore.

On Monday nights we all know that there
are free concerts at the Village Gazebo —
or do we? Newcomers and oldtimers
may need reminding that the concert series
sponsored by Village Recreation Department
is one of the top ten reasons we live here.
This coming Monday night (July 14) bring your
lawn chairs or blankets. Featured performers
will be young Village High School graduates.
In case of rain, the concert will be held at
the Town House. See you there!

JULY is the Month most like champagne.
JULY is the Month that goes to your head.

The July inside
Every cell in the human body
is charged by .01 volt of electricity per nanometer. That's
the life force! Equal to 20 million volts per yard!
The same amount of power generated within the body of a
thunderstorm. In other words, we are *lightning*. We
are made from the same stuff that ignites the
FIVE FORMS of FIRE
in every July night.

July 1

Conditions are favorable for severe weather is the forecast for today. In other words:

Welcome to July!

July 2

What a storm last night! In the midst of it at 2:00 AM I was in the alley calling for the stray cat who has so far resisted my attempts to turn him into a house cat. This was my chance to bring Louie inside once and for all but it was *thrilling* to be out there, in the lightning and the rain and even *I* didn't want to come in!

July 4   American Independence Day

Every July night is a star garden of constellations, and tonight there will be fireworks, reminding us of how it must have looked when the universe was born.

July 6

Ten years ago today I was a wanderer on a cold beach at midnight in Western Scotland. Something that night made me turn around and head home, even though I didn't know where that was. . . until I came here, two weeks later, and knew I'd be staying put for a while.

July 9

Today's the day! 100°! This is a fine and Fahrenheit distinction that 37 Celsius can't make. 37C covers a range of heat from 98.6 to 100° and that's just *pitiful* because: 98.6 is poetry, 99° is sexy, and 100° is *HOT*.

July 10

Another 100° day. I pride myself on my ability to tolerate heat. What's my secret? All I need is a ball gown and a little champagne.

July 15

When my cats hide under the kitchen table, wild eyed, ears flattened, wary — I know that there's a *monster* thunderstorm coming our way.

July 17

Now that the cicada bugs have hatched out of their underground burrows the heat will be *terrible*. For the next month the air will throb with their dreadful mating calls, shriek and buzz with the din of their creepy insect needs.

July 22

If you've ever wondered what a headache sounds like, come to the Long Island Sound in July. It's the sound of cicadas, seething in the air like a migraine as big as the sky.

July 25

It is a hot, hot night, too hot to sleep. Oh, if only I had a better pillow, made of snow and violets, I could rest, and dream of January.

July 29

I saw it coming, the break in the weather this afternoon. First, thunderclouds darkened the far side of the Village. Then a cold wind made the air chilly. Everything became hushed-BOOM! A crack of lightning and, finally, relief sheeted down in cool, quenching rain.

July 31

By day, the hiss and rattle of millions of ugly cicada bugs vexes my nervous system. *Ah,* but after sundown, that's when those brilliant flirts, the fireflies, come out. Those gentle blinking lights that they send to each other, so many tiny heartbeats of desire — they make the night bright in one of the **five** forms of fire that light up the July sky.

The CICADA has the longest life of any insect. It spends 13 to 17 years underground before it emerges in the night to climb up a tree and shed its skin, unfold its new wings, and make a noise that will attract a mate before it dies in 60 days. CICADAS in numbers can produce a noise that has been measured at 120 decibels. This is the threshold of **PAIN** to humans, similar to the sound of a chainsaw, or **THUNDER**.

Champagne and Ball Gowns
KEEP ME HAPPY IN CICADA SEASON

My mother said we looked like rag pickers. You see, it took a teenager's **keen eye** to tell the difference between **actual rags** and the ripped jeans, the patched-up hand-me-down peasant blouses, and the worn-out moccasins that were the height of high school chic in 1973. Even **if** the Senior Class at the Earl J. Wooster High School *had* held a Prom, no one would have gone. **Proms** were as **un-cool** as Richard Milhous **Nixon**.

I'm my mother's age now and I *want* to wear pretty dresses. This coppery-pink gown with shoulder straps made of strings of crystal "diamonds" is my **It's never too late to wear a Prom Dress** dress.

We'd lingered too long over our pre-show champagne cocktails so now we'd have to dash across midtown to get to the theater on time. **I**, in my Prom Dress, led the way down 43rd Street to Broadway. The Theater District is patrolled by the **NYPD Mounted Unit**, and an officer atop a huge chestnut-colored quarter horse kindly stopped traffic so I could race my companions through the gridlock. I waved thank you to him, and he bowed to me from his steed and called out, "**Miss, you look like a real lady tonight.**"

My 17-year-old self would have died from embarrassment. My 45-year-old self *glowed* the rest of the night. (I also love it when I'm not called **Ma'am**.)

Two things create a woman,
PRETTY DRESSES and *Love Letters*

Honoré de Balzac
Pere Goriot, 1835

right

I've never been a bridesmaid. I'm not complaining.
But when I bought this frock from the consignment shop I
justified the expense by telling myself that one day it **will**
come in handy, when one of my friends has an impromptu
wedding with come-as-you-are bridesmaids and I **just**
happen to be wearing yards and yards of this tulle
with a strapless, fitted bodice adorned on the back with
a big pink bow. However, since the skirts are
ballerina (Sugar Plum Fairy) length, and because
one night I **happened** to be wearing it at home
to re-arrange my tea cup collection while listening
to the only classical record I own, I call this my
TCHAIKOVSKY DRESS

left IN PRAISE OF PETTICOATS

In and out of style for the past 100 years, petticoats had their
baroque heyday in the couture of the 1950s chanteuse. I
bought this dress for $7.00 at a thrift shop because it had
formidable '50s petticoats; starched, stiff, and ruffled. I
ripped off the original puffy sleeves to turn it into this
off-the-shoulder dress that looked *fabulous* when I
jitterbugged. This dress won me First Prize at a fancy
dress party in Greenwich, CT. Every other gal wore a
poodle skirt — but the judge was a petticoat fan!

He had never seen anything to compare with her.

What was her name, her home, her life, her past? He longed to know the furniture in her room,

ALL THE DRESSES SHE HAD EVER WORN.

Gustav Flaubert
Sentimental Education, 1869

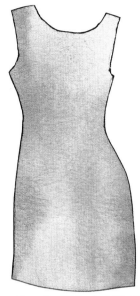

The French knew so much more about love and dresses than we did in the Philadelphia suburbs in the 1970s. That's why I took notes when I read their great novelists; because I was *finally* getting to the truth about life. I was 19 years old. I didn't suspect that literature could be full of irony and satire.

above

MY REWARD FOR TURNING 40

If not for this dress, I would never have had the nerve to date younger men. ～ I'd never been 40 before, and I had no experience acting my age. But I figured it was time for me to own at least one mature outfit. I let the salesgirl in a fancy dress shop pick out this beige dress for me. What's more mature than beige? The dress was made of an elegant rayon moiré and I doubted I'd fit into the tiny size 6 I was given to try on. Amazingly, the thing slid on me like dew on a rose petal, like inspiration on a non-ironic French novelist's woman.

So when I started meeting men I wished I'd met when I was in my 20s I'd wear this dress and let *them* deal with the age difference.

right

LAS VEGAS WEDDING DRESS

Vintage black mini-dress from the '60s, the last time cocktails were taken seriously as a dress occasion, when **Sin City** was a destination for *jet setters*, when sex was for adults only. This is the dress I'll wear the next time I get married: *Midnight in a chapel on the Strip* ～ *a blue suede jump-suited Elvis officiating.* And of course it will be 100° and it will be JULY.

① My 1st fiancé was a Californian I met in Paris.
② My 1st husband was a Gemini I met in the Levant.
③ My 2nd fiancé believed in long engagements —

—but after a year and a half I had to insist, "It's time to set a date." "O.K.," he said, as if agreeing. "Here's a list of things you have to change about yourself before I can marry you."

Oh sure, that's funny *now*, but at the time I was not amused.

I have a special place I go when my love life falls apart: **Scotland.**

This is the third time I've come here. The beaches **here** are good for the soul.

The Highlands of Scotland

RHUM

EIGG

The view

Camusdarach

For Scotland I took with me this man's linen jacket that an old boyfriend left behind in my closet. In the left pocket I carried a small pebble of pure white quartz from the hills near Camusdarach. The pebble was how I imagined the icy core of a **comet** would look. There was, this July, a very beautiful comet orbiting Jupiter,* spiraling down, in fact, on a collision course with the planet. For the first time in human history we would observe the phenomenon of bodies in our solar system slamming into one another. One astronomer spoke for all stargazers when he said, "It's a great time to be alive!"

Yes it is. **Every day, yes it is.**

* Shoemaker-Levy 9

Midnight in Scotland
on the road to
Camusdarach Beach

Camusdarach Beach
56:57 North Latitude

There is a lack of moonlight in the Highlands in July. Night does not fall here, this time of year. This is the time of the "Summer Dim" in Scotland. Due east, in Moscow, they're calling this a *white night*.

In the chilly midnight dusk I walk a mile to get to the sea coast. Alone on the beach I turn my back to the wind and I dig myself a seat in the sand dune. In the pockets of my jacket I've brought a picnic of crackers (slightly damp and gritty from the sea mist) and whisky (Oban Single Malt). The horizon here is famous for its view. The mountains on the western islands of Rum and Eigg are dark outlines in the pearly glow of the all-night twilight.

I'm going to admire the scenery here tonight, and hum pop songs from 10 years ago, from when there was great stuff on the radio.

I'm 38 years old. I can wait until tomorrow to figure out what to do with the rest of my life.

Two weeks later I will find myself looking at the shore of the Long Island Sound thinking, "Hmmm...maybe this is where I could **stay put.**"

When I was little

we called them LIGHTNING BUGS

Fireflies is the fancy word

At the end of the day I still go where they can be found at twilight, in the borderlands between **LAWNS** and **WOODS**

where their

MATING QUEST

begins.

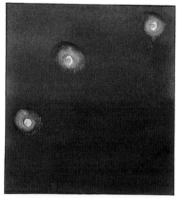

YOU

GAUDY GLOW WORM
carrying seeming fire
Yet have no heat
within Me

John Fletcher
(1579-1625)

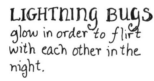

LIGHTNING BUGS

glow in order to flirt with each other in the night.

Stand in the cool grass in the dark and watch their gentle signals, calling to each other in random glitters of light. Something in our ancient animal brain responds to their search for a mate, and our hearts beat *faster,* in time with theirs.

At elegant garden parties in old **JAPAN** it was a sign of the host's **REFINEMENT** to set loose hundreds of **FIREFLIES** in the air for the amusement of his guests.

For special occasions tribesmen in **NEW GUINEA** wear live **FIREFLIES** in their hair.

Starlight falls to Earth in measurable quantities. Every minute, 1/10,000th ounce covers a square mile. ∼ See that shimmer on every blade of grass? That's a dusting of starlight.

THE EGYPTIANS imagined that the stars were lanterns let down by the gods from the sky ceiling to make the night sky more beautiful.

THE CHINESE called it THE PURPLE FORBIDDEN ENCLOSURE and mapped 283 constellations. They also discovered sun spots, calling them GUEST STARS.

THE BABYLONIANS believed that stars were the written words of a HEAVENLY LANGUAGE. Of their 48 constellations, the most important were the 12 of the ZODIAC.

There are approx. 4,000 stars visible to the naked eye.

Even now, when I know that those stars have all been named and numbered, explained, and classified, I feel that I am seeing the universe for the first time on these hot and starry nights.

The THIRD FORM OF FIRE *Nature's fireworks*

There are 2,000 lightning storms on the planet at any given moment, discharging 10 to 30 **MILLION** volts of electricity

100 strikes each second

Each bolt less than an inch thick.

Each bolt **FIVE TIMES** hotter than the surface of the sun

RECKLESS

JULY is a lightning brew. HOT air currents, LOW pressures, atmospheres rising and falling, all those 100,000,000,000 electrons rubbing up against each other, the agitated particles striking the earth in bolts that kindle the molecules that lie on the surface of this planet. Everywhere you go you get the feeling that the ground you walk on is not at rest, and the sky above is not at ease. It's enough to make you want to *RUN WILD.*

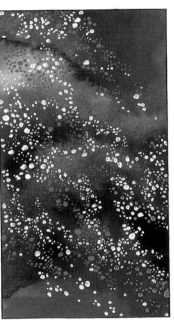   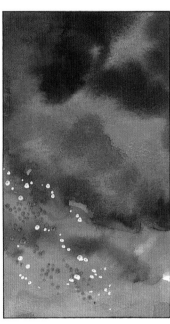

Fireworks

Falling Moons
Silver Flowers
Peonies strung on a thread
Lotus sprinkled with water
Lanterns of Heaven and Earth

Tun Li-chen, 1900
naming fireworks in his book
The Annual Customs & Festivals in Peking

In Japanese *fireworks* are called
hanabi ～ FIRE FLOWERS

in Chinese they are
花火 SMOKE FLOWERS

Irish
tinte ealaíne FIRE ART

Persian
atesh bazi FIRE GAME

Esperanto ARTFAJRAJO

A charm
7 days
a window
a gown of half magic
perfume
a pillow of small favors
the start of a wish
2 keys

There is never
only one explanation

CLOSE YOUR EYES
Open a book at random. Point to anyplace on the page.
Collect the words at your fingertips.
Repeat until you've gathered a TO DO list.

114

The FIFTH FORM OF FIRE

Summer Mind

Ah, a spell of coolness at last. The night is **78°** ～ "skin temperature", when the nerves on the surface of the body can't detect the boundary between the self and the surrounding atmosphere. Under such conditions, when a person dances under the stars there will be no telling where the soul ends and the universe begins.

August

The Wanderer's Rest
Summer Cafe

DAWN

When Summer cools down, becomes less like July and a little bit more like September, the days feel so much more *eventful*. It's not that so much happens in August ⌒ nothing much really *happens* in any one month ⌒ but whatever *does* happen in August feels like it might be the last happening of its kind. It's the **Last Chance** effect of the end of Summer, and every last little thing is eventful.

Especially at dawn. I take this last chance to walk through my Village in the hour before dawn and in the early light I feel like I'm the original tourist in this strange, wonderful place that is my every day life.

AUGUST is a FOREIGN COUNTRY

Coming face to face with robbers in Africa, keeping my eye on the guns pointed at me across the Jordan River, smuggling diamond jewelry out of South America (I was doing a friend a favor) — these *thrills* of travel are what I'm trading to stay put here, in my Village. To walk on any street, in the wee hours, in the dark, even, and know that I am **perfectly safe** is why I stay put in August.

I walk in the cool remnants of the night so I can hear myself think. The only part of an August day that has peace and quiet is the hour before dawn. Once the sun rises, the bugs warm up, and the racket of the multitudes drowns out my own thoughts.

So I get up before the bugs do. In these early dawn moments is where you find August.

Catch it while you can.

It was 4 o'clock in the morning and I was out walking in the dewy silence. I wandered to the edge of the meadow. Tumbling alongside me, at a little distance, was a white sheet of paper — maybe it was a windblown scrap. It seemed to be keeping pace with me. I was amused, and I smiled at this strange piece of litter bouncing along with me, matching my every step. It almost seemed to be hopping, as if it had a mind of its own.

In a sudden shift of light (the light is always shifting suddenly at that hour) the scrap of litter CAME ALIVE. In the first light of day I saw the white object materialize into the white cotton tail of a wild bunny. A rabbit out of thin air! As silently as if he were still invisible, the bunny loped beside me for another moment or two, before he turned sharply into the tall grass and, in an instant, disappeared.

August.

August 1

In August, get up at 4:00 AM and make your first cup of tea of the day. Make it sweet, with a drop of vanilla extract added in. Take this with you for your walk, outside in the dark quiet. Sip your steaming tea while drinking in the cool orchid flavors of the dawn.

August 3

The streets of my village look so foreign at 4:00 AM. The shop fronts, their public faces now shadowed by the peculiar silence of this time of day, look as mysterious to me as the stone heads on Easter Island.

August 6

If you wake up early enough you can join the squirrels for breakfast in the woods, you with your vanilla tea, them with their Rose of Sharon flower petal crêpes.

August 8

Walking through the woods this morning I almost stepped on a small white flower, rung 'round by the smallest fence I've ever seen ～ a daisy chain made of pipe cleaners. I thought all day about this "one weed" secret garden. It **must** be the work of either pixies, I figure, or wee space aliens.

August 11

Our mayor announced a Village milestone achievement this month: **37 years of fatality-free pedestrianism.** This is how we celebrate our own uneventfulness.

August 14

Shhhhh...For whole minutes at a time the cicada din quiets down, from the sound of a chainsaw to the dull roar of the ocean.

August 16

Today was the same as yesterday, which was the same as the day before and the day before that: cool in the morning, hot by mid-day, rain in the afternoon, a warm night. Some people complain about being bored this time of year, the August Lull. It's another lost art : knowing **how to abide the lull.**

August 20

Summer passes so quickly. Even the rain was in a hurry today. The weather pushed into town like it was in a temper and got all the leaves on the trees riled up, and then it fired a barrage of water droplets out of the sky, heavy plops of rain, poking me all over.

August 23

Summer passes so quickly: there are wool sweaters on display in the dress shop window. And even worse, pinned up behind them are big paper cutouts in the shape of Fall leaves and snowflakes.

August 25

A change is in the air. It smells woody and leafy, different from the Summery scent of flowers and hot pavement. Could this be the first sign that Summer is ending?

August 29

A change in the sound of the evening. Instead of the drone of cicadas, there is the hush of crickets. There's no doubt now that the end of Summer is *here.*

August 31

The alarm rang at 4:00 AM. It was dark, as usual, but it was **chilly**. I didn't want to get up. So I slept *late* and I got up long after sunrise.
That's how I said Good-bye to August.

THE WEEKLY NEWS

The streets of the Village were so quiet this last week of late August that you could roll a bowling ball down Main Street and not hit a parked car — and you can attend the free weekly concert at the Gazebo and have "front row seats."

Street Sign Pointing Wrong Way

On Aug. 5, Village police received a report that a one-way sign on Third Avenue was moved and pointing the wrong way. Officers corrected the sign's placement.

It's August.
Pull up a chair and Summer Lull with me.

A MEMOIR of CLOSE CALLS
in Three Minuscule Chapters

1. Africa

The good thing about a military dictatorship is that it cuts down on street crime. In Niamey, Niger, in the 1980s, Colonel Seyni Koutché had a thousand armed soldiers on patrol in the city, and petty thievery lost its appeal as a career path among ne'er do wells. By god we felt safe. All we had to beware of was malaria, leprosy, hepatitis B, polio, spinal meningitis, shistosomiasis, typhoid, river blindness, sleeping sickness, and the next military coup.

So when I was mugged one night I was more indignant than afraid. The boys had surrounded me, muttering their threats. Then one of them grabbed my purse and they all ran away. They stole my month's spending money, but that wasn't my worst problem.

I had my 100% all-natural boar bristle hairbrush in my purse. In this part of the world, 100% all-natural boar bristle hairbrushes are *irreplaceable*. And heaven knows how hard Africa is on your hair without top-of-the-line hair care products. I was furious! I ran after the thieves and almost tripped over the contents of my purse on the roadside, the trinkets and cosmetics that the theives had scattered after themselves. And there was my hairbrush! Right next to my priorities.

2. South America

The Duchess's great-great-great nephew, an unpublished poet living in São Paulo, asked me to smuggle the heirloom diamond necklace past Brazilian Customs on my way home to New York. Experts at a famous auction house there were eager to put the necklace into their next sale of "Magnificent Jewels". The Duchess, who knew Lord Byron intimately, would have been amused.

At the time, I was in the business of selling Imperial Fabergé, Incan emeralds, and flawless diamonds. I was used to carrying valuables in my pockets or, as in this case, hidden under my turtleneck sweater. The poet hailed a taxi for me and, without a thought, I hopped into the back seat for the 25 km ride to Guarulhos Aeroporto.

It was a mistake to get into the car. I realized this as soon as it dawned on me that I was alone with a stranger in a city of 20 million inhabitants notorious for their poverty and violence, where people get killed for a few dollars — and I had 30 diamonds around my neck. I could barely breathe as I stared out of the backseat window, in terror, searching the dark highway for signs that we were heading towards the bright lights of an airline terminal and not down some shady side street towards my obituary. When I finally saw the silhouette of an airplane on the horizon I almost fainted with relief.

These days, in my little village on the Long Island Sound, I hardly ever have to worry about getting home alive.

Suitcase CAT BED

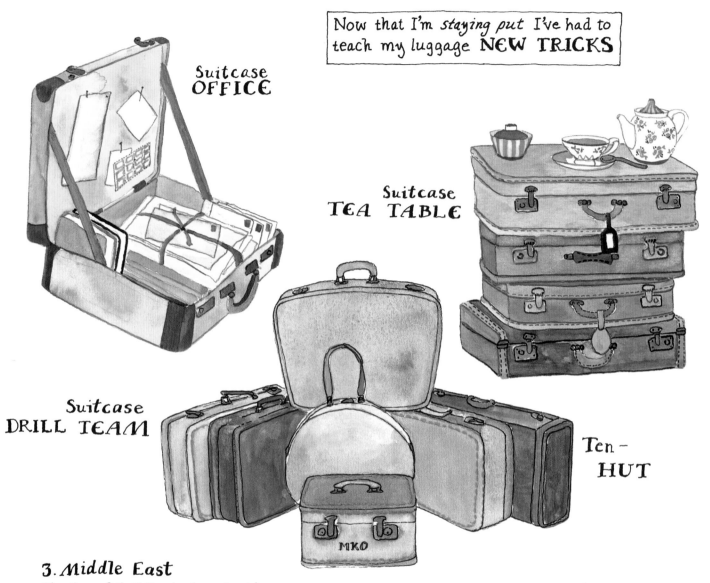

Now that I'm *staying put* I've had to teach my luggage NEW TRICKS

Suitcase OFFICE

Suitcase TEA TABLE

Suitcase DRILL TEAM

Ten-HUT

MKO

3. Middle East

The Great Rift Valley is where the African continent has pulled itself apart from the Asian landmass creating a 4500-mile rip in the Earth's crust that starts in northern Syria and ends in central Mozambique. The Jordan River meanders through the deepest part of the rift, in the valley between the Galilee and the Dead Sea.

I liked to stand on the west bank of the Jordan River near Tiberius, with my back to the setting sun, to watch the play of light on the ancient dusty canyon walls of the Jordanian highlands. The Arabian Army protects this stretch of the river border of the Hashemite Kingdom, and as I watched the warm sandstone cliffs glow in the cool violet dusk I could see the soldier on the other side stand alert, his rifle at the ready. From my perch on enemy territory, I'd wave *shalom*. He'd wave back, *salaam*.

After my walk at dawn I go back home to make myself a second cup of tea and to wake up my old house cat, Woody Robinson. We tippy-toe out to our back alley. Our stray cat friend, Louie, meets us there.

No one ever goes back here ⌒ it's an **alley**. So every day for an hour it's *all ours*, our very own country, a land-locked nation with no major roads, no industry, no army, no crime. A nation where the chief activity of the population is to not disturb the August Lull. The boys hunt for beetles and laze in the shade of the cornstalks. I re-read old diaries and make drawings of the herb gardens I'll plant one day.

Climate Zones in the MicroNation of Pawsylvania

The start of a new day in the alley: hot tea, French honey, vanilla from Madagascar.

In the vegetable garden, dew dries off the ears of corn (smells like clean sheets), fresh raked dirt still scented by yesterday's rain.

Baking in the sun: black-eyed susans on the other side of the fence and tree bark: there's an appetizing aroma of melting caramel and Islay Scotch in the air.

Old softwood trees: the smell of parchment and damp cement whenever a breeze ruffles the half-dead pine needles.

Cool shadows left over from the night, held in place by broad-leafed deciduous trees. Blue jays nest here ⌒ a jay perches on a low branch and scolds the cats for trespassing in his territory (that's where the shade is). Notes of leather, chocolate, faded velvet, old library books.

Louie, Woody Robinson, and Me

in our own little *world*

Some moments in time have **borders** that separate them from all the other weeks and months of your life. I thought I'd always have Augusts like that August, when I spent all those hours in the alley with my cats in our own little world. But by the next year Woody was withdrawn deep into the far corners of his own world of old age and ill health (he was gone by September) and in the meantime Louie had reverted to his vagabond ways and we never saw him again. But I know the way back. And I'll travel there, back in time, again and again, for as long as I live.

August. Catch it while you can.

I recognize Louie's chirp, his call for me to come quick! He has a present for me! Another freshly caught mouse. He does a dance, hopping and prancing in a circle around me, anticipating my praise.

Later, when he is taking a victory nap in the sun, I will lay the little rodent body to rest in the **Mouse Burial Grounds** (see above).

125

Micronations like us

MICRONATIONS

are small, self-declared state-like entities existing in real or imagined space (some even issuing **PASSPORTS**, minting **COINS**, printing **STAMPS**, and awarding **NOBLE TITLES**) which **DO NOT** meet any international criteria for **STATEHOOD**.

Their **Highnesses** the **MOST SERENE AND USUALLY NAPPING Lords of Pawsylvania** Woody the Robinson and Louie I with the First Lady & Prime Minister of Civility and Decorum (me)

The **Republic of Rose Island Government in Exile** (official language: ESPERANTO) perpetuates the sovereignty of a 1200-square-foot floating platform in the *Adriatic Sea* that DISAPPEARED in 1968 when it was **BLOWN UP** by the **ITALIAN NAVY**

The **PRINCIPALITY** of **SEALAND**, located in **international waters** (6 miles off the east coast of England, has no land mass *per se*, being a **World War II PONTOON** the size of a baseball diamond, but has *never-the-less* inspired protracted "discussion" in the **EUROPEAN Union** over the right of artificial islands to self-determination.

The Hutt River Principality is AUSTRALIA's *oldest* micronation, having declared its independence on **April 21, 1970**. Its **KNIGHTHOODS** were on sale throughout Europe but the practice was terminated so the **PRINCIPALITY** could celebrate it 30th **ANNIVERSARY** in 2000 with **DIGNITY**.

Passport

PAWSYLVANIA

NOT SO MUCH A PLACE AS ANOTHER TIME

GIVEN LEAVE TO LINGER
PAWSYLVANIA
FOR AS LONG AS YOU DON'T MAKE A NUISANCE OF YOURSELF

THE MAIL COMES IN ON LITTLE CAT FEET

PAWSYLVANIA

Talossa, a KINGDOM founded in 1979 by a teenager in his Milwaukee bedroom, has its own language with approx. 90 speakers world-wide. A *breakaway republic* was declared in 2000 by CITIZENS who thought some people were taking it all too seriously, or *maybe* not seriously *enough*. **Other factions** have annexed Talossan territory in *Antarctica* and the French island of **Cezembre**.

LADONIA consists of **2** DRIFTWOOD SCULPTURES on a beach in southern **SWEDEN** and a collection of "nomads" (citizens) ～ an **international group of artists** who PROTECT Ladonia from the Swedish authorities' *years-long* effort to have the DRIFTWOOD "sculptures" REMOVED.

Not valid on guilt trips

No Wuddas·Shuddas·Cuddas

REMEMBRANCE

YOUR TICKET TO THE PAST

A whiff of vanilla
The taste of penny candy
A favorite song from 20 years ago
The first cool breeze of Fall
Your mother's favorite color

USE IT TO GO SOME PLACE NICE WHY DON'T YOU

My Village toe-holds 2.47 sq. miles onto the Long Island Sound, all that remains from the original "purchase" of 9,000 acres from the Siwanoy Algonquin Indians in 1654. A walk down the Main Street is as good as visiting a curious foreign land, and here are some of the reasons why:

Often found in the first syllable of many Village landmarks *(see right)* the **PELICAN** is our civic symbol, since the coat of arms from the first **LORD** of the **Manor**, 1666. The pelican here *(see below)* is on the old lanterns on the **BANK BUILDING** ∽ built 1929 and closed on the famous Bank Holiday of March 4, 1933, the last **panic** of the Great Depression.

The Bank is now our Post Office.

above: the "Gothik" doorknob from the Pelnord's front entrance.

The president of the Village Bank, Mr. John T. Brook, was found guilty of using $125,000 of the bank's money to play the stock market. He was sentenced to 5 years in prison. Mr. Brook was a respected local business-man, having built the Pelnord Apartments in 1923, using the **TUDOR** style so as to signify that life in our Village was **CLASSY**: the apartments had window casements from England, cheval glass from France, and oak flooring from Tennessee.

A Tour of my *Village* ∽
a **MICRONATION** on the Long Island Sound

above
Tudor architecture,
Renaissance Man within

left
This **Memorabilia Still Life** has been in the window of the vegetable stand on Main Street for all the 10 years that I've lived here. The stand rarely has paying customers ∽ mostly, townspeople stop here to discuss politics with the owner, who is the chairman of the Village's Republican Party.

The Lull in Conversation

It's so predictable (it happens every seven minutes) that the French have a saying for that 8th minute of silence: *Shhhh*, they say, *an angel is passing by.*

The year is like a conversation.
Then an angel passes by.
Her name is *AUGUST*.

0 decibels (dB) is the threshold of human hearing, which is a sound that is approximately that of a mosquito in flight a yard away. Any sound less than 20 dB is QUIET

Breathing

A whisper

Rustling leaves

A wind chime from the next block

Turning the pages of an old diary

The clink of ice cubes in a glass of Long Island Iced Tea

Someone sweeping their porch with a broom

Dealing cards for a game of solitaire

Laughing to yourself, over a joke, remembered from a long time ago

The breeze at dawn has secrets to tell you.
Don't go back to sleep.

Rumi
Persian Poet, 1207 - 1273

SEPTEMBER

Hemingway, F. Scott Fitzgerald, & ME
℅ 8, Rue Scribe

It used to be that the overseas offices of American Express would hold mail for any customer who bought AmEx's traveler's checks ~ even grubby backpackers who only cashed $20 at a time. Just **one** American Express traveler's check entitled you to use their London or Paris address as your own. Collecting a long-awaited letter from home at the splendid **Rue Scribe** offices or from the historic **Haymarket** edifice (around the corner from Piccadilly Circus) made my homesickness just a little bit *glamorous*.

Staying Put: Now that I get my mail at my own permanent address I hardly ever get homesick at all.

The trees are still lush with greenery and they rustle as if they are still full of juicy leaves, but the breeze is different. It's cool, and efficient in a way that a Summer breeze is not. A September breeze is on its way somewhere, has things to do.

It bustles with a "Let's get this over with" rush. I must remember this for when, in the long dark months ahead, the bare trees have become silent and this sound of wind-tossed leaves is almost impossible to imagine.

September.   A Light or So Less.

Postcards were the instant messages of the 1970s. I sent 5 or 6 a day on my first hitch-hiking trip through England and France. I was 20. I fascinated myself. Why wouldn't my fellow Americans, marooned at home, be equally captivated by everything I had to say about my discovery of the **OLD WORLD**? As a brand new **traveler** and **sophisticate**, I had **savoir faire** to spare.

Now 20 years later, a stranger in this little Village on the Long Island Sound, I am searching for a stay-put serenity to replace my brash wanderer's self-satisfaction.

What I found was this battered picture post card of the Eiffel Tower, early one September morning (the weather was cool, but dewy), in the grass along a quiet side street not far from my new address. The postmark was over 20 years old, from the 8th arrondissement in Paris — the same post office I used when I lived in Paris in my mid-20s. Dated Feb. 20, 1974, this was the message:

Dear Steve —
Gas + fuel shortage not as apparent here as in London — although there may be a light or so less. Hope you're fine.
— Dad

Let me remind you what 1974 was like:

The *shortage* mentioned here is the **energy crisis** resulting from the Arab oil embargo of the United States and our allies for supporting Israel in the Yom Kippur War of 1973. In London, a coal miners' strike and austerity measures to conserve fossil fuels mandated a three-day work week that led to a 40% pay cut for 15 million workers and massive unemployment. Shops in the capital were lighting candles and gas lamps to stay in business.

In the U.S. gasoline rationing and sky-rocketing prices at the pump (from 30¢ a gallon in September to $1.20 by February) put the economy in a severe recession. In February the Dow was crashing toward a 45% total decline.

1974. My first year out of high school, working at my first job in the office of a factory in the suburbs of Philadelphia. I thought I was living the death of the American Dream. I was sure I'd never leave the factory, never escape the suburbs, never get to live in Paris. To make things worse, the song *Seasons in the Sun* by Terry Jacks was on every radio station *all the time*. *Seasons in the Sun* was the creepy, droning, brain-damagingly catchy, vaguely-about-death *monster hit* of the year.

I HATED 1974.

A Light or So Less, the traveler wrote. Now *that's* **savoir faire.**

September 1

Sure it's still Summer, but already the morning seems to be dimmer and the shade feels a bit cooler. It's these little changes that, every September, make a **BIG** difference to me.

September 6

The sound of the twilight has changed. No more cicadas, they've all mated and buried their eggs underground and died. Now it's cricket time. The crickets call to each other in singing as sweet as night-cold honey. In between their songs, in the silence from moment to moment, Summer takes its leave.

September 8

Three letters in my mail today! A real letter is a rare treat these days but **3** in one day restores my hopes for the future of humanity.

September 11

Red sky in the morning, sailors and citizens take warning. The dawn was blood-orange ~ because of a hurricane in the Gulf of Mexico, 1000 miles to the south, pushing stormy weather into the Long Island Sound today.

September 12

The 2nd day of pouring rain. It's still not too late to take one more walk in the rain ~ I gladly ruined a pair of shoes in the flash flood on Main Street, drenching myself in the end of Summer.

September 13

Brilliant, clear blue morning. What's left of the hurricane is heading for Maine. I hope they appreciate it up there.

September 17

I had to put on a sweater for my walk this morning ~ LONG SLEEVES!

September 19

My neighbor rescued a kitten that was dumped out of a passing car today and came to me : this kitten is the ugliest thing I've ever seen. She has a scrunched-up face like a fruit bat, beady eyes like a lemur, and a ratty fur coat the color of road kill. Of course I loved her at first sight.

September 20

Today our Nature Center releases the inhabitants of its Butterfly House. Home to six native species (to save them from extinction), the Center throws all its doors open at the end of Summer and sets every butterfly free to die "wild". Why does September have to be so sad?

September 21

This is it, the final day of Summer. I watched the sun go down and I found that I was holding my breath. The light faded, as did a little part of my heart.

September 26

There was a bite in the crisp air today! A thrilling briskness that I'd forgotten since last year, something about how Fall makes me feel wide awake and keen for a *change*.

September 30

I wrote letters all day, sharing my news about putting a heavier Fall blanket on my bed, my new kitten, a dream I had in French... This is my **acre of Earth**, I'm the only one who can describe it to the rest of the world.

Three things a wise person should know, just for reference points: the weighty heft of 24 karat gold, the playful wit in Nancy Mitford's letters, and the 43,560-square-foot swath of an acre of Earth.

I know pure gold when I hold it. I know epistolary perfection when I read it. A land surveyor friend today took me to the cemetery and paced off 209 feet × 209 feet, so now I'll know an **acre** when I see it.

P.S. It's *much* bigger than I thought.

The Acre of Earth Theory of Life

- Everybody gets an acre of Earth when they're born.
- Parents are the first fences.
- Teenagers think that ugly clothes, uglier hairstyles, and horrible music tears down those fences. This is pretty funny.
- Whatever you do in your 20s is just mapping expeditions.
- By the time you're 35 you're probably a battle weary veteran of numerous clashes over territory, a few border wars ⟶ your acre of Earth's been trampled pretty bad. It could use some re-landscaping.
- It takes most of your 40s to clear out the dead wood, plant a nice garden, dredge the swampy bits, observe the seasons. This is how you discover that there's an Eden on the far side of your acre that you *never knew was there.*

If you **EVER** feel crowded into a corner by your life, you need to take a better look at your acre of Earth. **IT'S BIGGER THAN YOU THINK.**

End of Summer
21 Days
September,
Every Year

a. Hubcap Diamond Star Halo

T-Rex, only the **best name for a rock band** *EVER*. The first hint of Fall makes me feel so *young*. Funny, so does wearing the oldest piece of clothing I own.

b. Football Season English Style is

from *August to May*, about the same amount of time I'll be wearing this **woolly** pullover with the Arsenal cannon on the hem. The kit shop at Highbury is as close as I got to the famous pitch that I'd read so much about in books by Johnny Rotten and Nick Hornby but wearing this sweater makes me feel like I'm with them in the North Bank stand screaming rude songs about Chelsea fans.

The First Sweaters of FALL

c. Long sleeves are so exciting! This vintage gypsy-peasant

acrylic knit sweater is *perfect* for this time of year, so **Back-to-School**, so much more about **fashion** than **warmth**. In the mid-1970s this is the kind of thing that would have been worn by a cheerleader going through a "hippie" phase.

Woolly Bear is the caterpillar form of the Isabella Tiger Moth. They are out and about in September, filling up on dandelions and maple leaves before they hibernate for the Winter. According to legend, the wider the woolly bear's middle section is, the milder the coming Winter will be.

Life sized. It's going to be a cold Winter.

**Scooter
the ugly kitten**

I made orange marmalade today. The thing about making marmalade is that you can't stir the boiling oranges (always **Seville**, in sugar water) with anything but a **wooden spoon**. No METAL, so say all the best marmalade makers in the world. But I didn't have a wooden spoon. I had a wooden ruler. So that's what I used.

My new kitten kept climbing onto the stove. No amount of shoo-ing kept her away from the flame, so I scooped her up and put her in the pocket of my apron. She settled down like a baby kangaroo.

It was while I was pouring the hot marmalade into jars to cool that I thought: of all the things that Earth's six billion people are doing tonight to keep busy, I am probably the **only person on the planet** making orange marmalade with a kitten in her pocket.

Acre of Earth Stuff

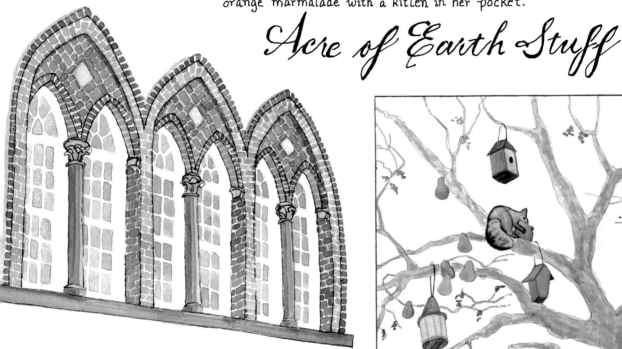

above
Windows of the Siwanoy Elementary School on the Long Island Sound the day before school starts.

right   Whatever kind of pear it is that grows on a tree that looks **dead** before it sprouts fruit in September, that's the kind of pear this fat squirrel is chewing on for breakfast.

PITTSBURGH PAINTS

WISE HARDWARE

Electrical · Plumbing · Maintenance & Garden
Power Tools · Vacuum · Glass & Screen Repairs

Keys

SKIL

More

Acre of Earth Stuff

The first week of September is hummingbird migration time on the **LONG ISLAND SOUND**. Ruby-throated Hummingbirds are on their way to **Central America** for the Winter and they stop here to feed on the last of the Summer flowers before they fly south. I read once that hummingbirds pull apart spider webs to use the silk threads to make their nests. **Whether** or **not** this is **True** this story has a place on my **acre of Earth**.

Being 21, riding on the back of a motorcycle with my arms wrapped around a 22-year-old French Buddhist who's wearing his grandmother's old fur coat and opal earrings, roaring down the *Champs Élysées* on an April night – *that* has a place in the **FRANCE** corner of my acre of Earth.

Coral-colored roses, white violets, and girls named Mary have a place on my acre of Earth.

I was 25, working in a bookstore on 5th Avenue. The big Irish college kid who stocked the shelves had a crush on me. He'd stare at me over the stacks to get my attention, then he'd sigh. One day he couldn't keep his admiration to himself and he said to me, "Vivian, if you were a dog, you'd be a collie." That boy has a place on my acre of Earth.

So does the Hell's Angel I met in Oakland, California (1973), who was reading *Gone With the Wind*.

Sandstorms on the Sahara share a place on my acre of Earth with Hurricanes in southern America and the Northern Lights in Alaska, the *Acts of God* I'd like to see Again place.

Champagne, CREAM SODA, A&W Root Beer, & white wine (with notes of Elmer's Glue & Fruit Loops) have a place in the bar on my acre of Earth.

Picking out embroidery floss for a new sewing project, deciding which stitches to use, cutting the fabric from a new bolt of cloth, threading the needle to begin: this has had a place on my acre of Earth since I was 10 years old.

1976 being the year that I discovered John Singer Sargent at the Philadelphia Museum of Art, I went to London and asked about one of his pictures at the Tate Gallery. "It's in storage," the curator said, "Come tomorrow and we'll take you to the vault." In the basement chamber, just because I'd asked, having a private audience with *CARNATION, LILY, LILY, ROSE* has a place in the **Dumb Luckiest Things That Ever Happened To Me** area of my acre of Earth.

Libraries before they took away the card catalog and put bar codes on the books **will always have a place on my acre of EARTH**.

My MUSEUM of LETTERS

top left I like my name in lights, sort of, on this letter from an artist friend.

middle left Vintage stamps on the last letter I ever got from the best friend I had in the Peace Corps. I don't know why he stopped writing.

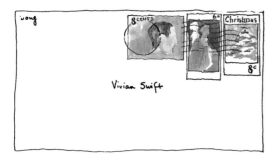

above English stamps on a Nottingham post mark, like charms on a bracelet.

below Found Letters from the Village

above When I bought a vintage Style Council LP on Ebay it arrived in a package with all these stickers on it, arranged like a Kurt Schwitters collage.

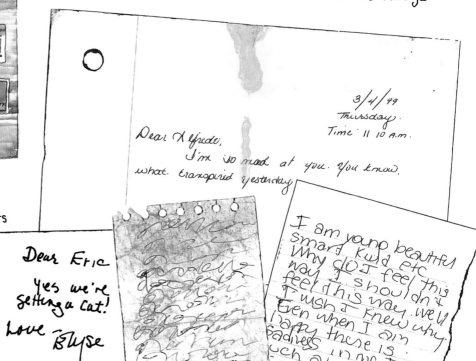

3/4/99
Thursday.
Time 11 10 A.M.

Dear Alfredo,
I'm so mad at you. You know what transpired yesterday

Dear Eric
Yes we're getting a cat!
Love Elyse

I am young beautiful smart kind etc. Why do I feel this way I shouldn't feel this way well I wish I knew why. Even when I am happy there is sadness in me...

LONDON
I love my hotel - its in a neighborhood with lots of cats.

SALISBURY
I saw a black kitty on my way to the cathedral this morning so I petted him. I plan to see Stonehenge later today.

IPSWICH
I took a bus to get here. My hotel is the most I've paid yet. I have a sore throat.

COLCHESTER
It got a little sunny today. I'm going to see Thomas Gainsboro's house (finally).

BATH
I bought some tea spoons and jelly dishes so I can fix us a proper "tea" when I get home. Send all mail to Paris from now on.

PARIS
A loaf of french bread cost 25¢!

GRENOBLE
I made it here from Dijon (spent night in Lyon). I had escargot (delicious) last night and I drank half a bottle of beaujolais!

RENNES
I've had a wonderful crêpes dinner with wine - lucky me!! and soon I will be in Clermont-Ferrand.

CARCASSONE
I prefer the Languedoc region to the Roman ruins I saw in Provence.

CHABLIS
Been visiting the vineyards. I might visit a frenchman I met on a train in Bordeaux.

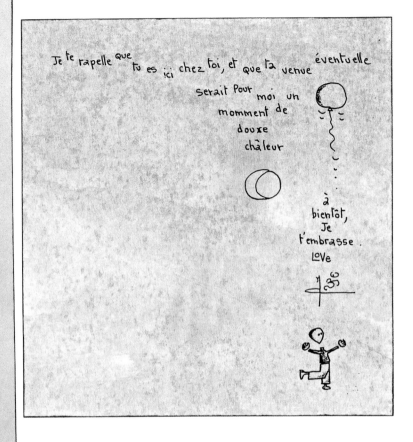

left: Excerps from my postcards, 1976, from my first travels through England and France.
P.S. That last note from Chablis was such a lie! I was just showing off (as usual) - I had no intention of accepting that French guy's invitation to visit him in Bordeaux. In fact, I was SHOCKED when he started FLIRTING with me. I was smitten with France, not Frenchmen, not yet, not like above, from my first French boyfriend, 1979.

My Museum of Letters is the biggest building on my Acre of Earth.
I also have a Warehouse of Grudges and
an Institute of All the Shades of Blue.

Words aren't all I have

I'll remember every morning that I've walked barefoot on grass that was soft and itchy — when snow falls into my socks over the tops of my boots when I take the same walk in December.

The kindly twinkling haze of the Big Dipper is what I'll remember, after the first frost, when the cold stars of Orion seem so far away.

I'll save my memory of reading my mail in the bright daylight for when I'll have to remember to turn on the porch light for the mailman's arrival in the afternoon twilights to come.

I love to watch how the day,
tired as it is,
lags away RELUCTANTLY,
AND HATES TO BE CALLED Yesterday so soon.

Nathaniel Hawthorne,
House of the Seven Gables, 1851

The Last of the Summer sunsets on the Long Island Sound

October

STAY PUT
Let the coyote come to you

By day, the Village and I seem unchanged. But at night, things are different. It's cooler, blacker, deeper, and mightier than the delicate sweet spell of darkness that is the nighttime in Summer.

OCTOBER is the
COYOTE Month

when the days prowl towards Winter and the nights become wild and cunning.

It is dark when I walk home from work now and I'm not used to it. I walk quickly to keep warm. The sidewalk is covered in fallen leaves that scuttle alongside my footsteps like friendly, living things, keeping me company on the lonely pavement. The wind is half warm, half cool, like breath from two kinds of beasts, one hot-blooded and one whose blood runs cold, following me.

Coyote weather.

It is October and there is change in the air, stalking the shadows of every sunset. You can feel it gaining strength, to shake loose every leaf on every tree, something dark and wild. Maybe it's just the night, getting longer and deeper every day. But maybe it's the Coyote, the trickster god who is alive and afoot in **October.**

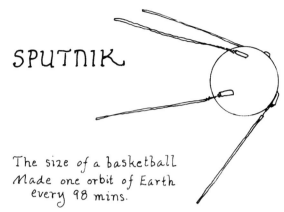

SPUTNIK

The size of a basketball
Made one orbit of Earth
every 98 mins.

Burned up on re-entry
on Jan. 4, 1958

October 4, 1957: those Soviet tricksters launch the first man-made satellite into Earth orbit. Russian stuff in *our* skies gave every red-blooded American the creeps. Already we were fighting a Cold War against their dastardly Communism. Now we jumped into a Space Race knowing we were a lap behind.

My single victory as a Space Racer was when I won a blue ribbon when I was 10 for decorating a game booth at my elementary school fair. The game, in which players squirted water pistols at lit candles that were set in aluminum foil rocket ships in orbit around a cardboard Earth, was called **Sputter the Sputnik**. I was *very* proud of winning my blue ribbon. I never won another school prize in my life. For this reason, Sputnik has always had a special place in my heart.

For almost 40 years I assumed that **Sputnik** was the name of some purely evil Communist god that stole our friendly heavens away from us. After all, the rockets that *we* sent up after it we named for the mythic deities of our mighty Western civilization, a slew of Cold War **Mercury**s, **Gemini**s, **Apollo**s, and **Saturn**s.

I just found out this year that **Sputnik** only means *traveler*. Far from launching a *god* to glorify their culture's mythological might, the Russians simply sent a little *traveler* up in the sky. So now it seems to me that our side over-reacted, got a little hysterical with our pompous nomenclature, with our divine Apollonian oracles and our Saturnian supreme ruler of the heavens. For Pete's sake, I want to say, CALM DOWN. And I want to say, Good night sweet Sputnik, wherever you are.

October 1

Wildness in the air, day and night. The change of season from Summer to Fall is drastic, thrilling, and threatening.

October 4

On this day in 1957 the Russians launched Sputnik, the first man-made satellite, into Earth orbit. Now, long after the Space Race is over, satellites passing overhead are an ordinary part of the night sky. It is cold and clear tonight when I walk outside to look at the Fall constellations. *Hi there, Orion.*

October 8

The heat came on in the house for the first time today. The radiators clanked and steamed, scattering the last atoms of Summer.

October 11

Unfallen rain was in the air this morning, darkening the day to a dim haze so that every color, of leaf, bark, grass, and brick, all look the same. I can't think of what to call this state of things, when everything has the same brownish-grey color.

Pelt of the Coyote?

October 14

A wild quince tree is a rare sight. There's only one in the Village, and I keep its location a secret lest someone be tempted to "tame" it. I went to admire my dear quince tree today — it's full of ridiculously bright yellow autumn-ripened fruit.

October 16

Cool, sunny, and blowsy. The wind rustles through piles of raked leaves, setting them loose to swirl away down the road with a whispery, scratching sound, scuttling like romping animals.

October 19

The locust tree on the corner is shedding long, slender yellow leaves. In the dark, in the halo of gold light from the street lamp, the leaves fall and spin and twirl through the air, each leaf flickering like a shard of mirrored light that glitters for an instant and then shivers into nothingness.

October 20

It's dark now at 6:30, a time that in Summer would be the golden part of the late after-noon. Now, it's the Witching Hour: the first hour after sun down that is as black as night, when witches roam.

October 23

Already the Christmas decorations are up in the stationery store!

October 25

A trip to the Cloisters today, a museum of medieval art, with a friend who has recently fallen deeply in love. A person in love is not the best company in ordinary situations, but in a religious art museum they are insufferable — every stained-glass saint and sacred relic reminded my friend of something he *must* tell me about his beloved.

October 27

It looks to me that *this* is THE DAY of PEAK leaf color on the shore of the Long Island Sound.

October 30

We set the clocks back to Standard Time today, so now the night falls *another* hour earlier. This is the hardest part of October, letting go of the light. No wonder the night feels so menacing, the way it has stolen into our afternoon hours like this.

The first Americans felt the presence of the COYOTE every day of their lives. Coyote myths exist in every Native American culture, stories of the Coyote as *Creator*, Messenger, HERO, or *Fool*. His most important guise is as the TRICKSTER, appearing in his ANIMAL, HUMAN, and SPIRIT forms to satisfy his Coyote nature: PLAYFUL LUSTY RECKLESS IMPULSIVE.

WHAT TO WEAR IN OCTOBER: FRINGE IS IN!

A Touch of the Coyote
It was Buffalo Bill's Wild West traveling show of the 1880s that brought the garments of the pioneer frontier to East Coast audiences, popularizing the fashions that would become synonymous with the **Old West**. *Back then* it was the fringed War Shirt of the Plains Indians. *In the 1970s* my fringed suede jacket was what I wore to clothe my coyote nature.

Red October
Eastern Woodland Indians living in the dense forest needed clothing that wouldn't get caught in the brush, that fit close to the body. It was the tribes living in the vast open plains – the Sioux, Comanche, Cheyenne– whose flowing garments, festooned with elk teeth, bear claws, feathers, and fringes became the iconic *look* of America. The big-shoulder look of the 1980s here supports the immense fringed shawl collar on my big red coat that any Plains warrior would recognize as *power dressing*.

Witching Hour White
Thrums is what American frontiersmen called the fringes on their Indian style shirts and leggings, for the noise their garments made, so many strips of leather *thrumming* with each movement of the body.
My 1990s mohair jacket is fringed with wisps of wool, and in it I am as silent as the owl that the Indians call "hush wings" in this new nocturnal life I lead in October.

on October 14, 1066
the Frenchman **William DUKE of NORMANDY**
defeated **HAROLD** the English King in a day-long
battle at **HASTINGS** to become
WILLIAM THE CONQUEROR King of England,
founder of a dynasty that rules to this day

VVILLEM REX

MOI When I was 10 years old *this* is how I
thought I'd look on my 30th birthday

What do you want to be when you grow up?

I was getting asked that *all the time* and I couldn't come up with a good answer. Of course, I was only 10 years old, and adults were only putting the pressure on me because they couldn't think of anything else to say to a kid; but still. I was a whole decade old and I didn't have a career path in the works. That's enough to give a kid an identity crisis.

It was the Summer of 1966. My parents believed that Day Camp, or arts and crafts classes, or play dates, or any organized activity whatsoever would just get in the way of a child keeping her own self busy from sun up to sun down, so I was pretty bored by the time the August issue of the National Geographic Magazine was delivered to the house. How else can I explain why the cover story, **The 900th Anniversary of the Norman Conquest,** got my attention?

I'd never heard of the Normans, their conquest of England, their hometown of Bayeux, or their native country, France.

The article inside the magazine was 45 pages long. I studied every photograph, and when I was finished I knew what I wanted to be when I grew up: **FRENCH**.

And *that*, as the poet said, *has made all the difference.*

The BAYEUX Stitch

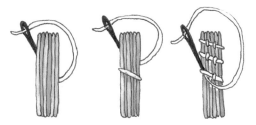

I taught myself to embroider from books which were all written for right-handed seamstresses.

I had to look at the illustrations upside down to figure out how to sew them left-handed.

This is how I sew.

If I had known the word **epiphany** when I was ten years old I would have used it to explain the **brain thunder** I felt when I first laid eyes on *The Bayeux Tapestry* as featured in the National Geographic Magazine of August 1966. The "tapestry" is a piece of embroidery a yard wide and 231 feet long that tells the picture story of the Norman Conquest of 1066, sewn by French needle-workers c.1070 — when the events of the French victory over the English kingdom was still fresh in their minds.

I've never gotten over my first impression of the Tapestry. It is narrative and visual perfection, a creation that sets the standards of **information** and **inspiration** for every other work of art that dares to call itself "art."

I've gone to Bayeux half a dozen times to see the Tapestry and to judge the long-term prospects of my accompanying significant others, according to their appreciation of it.

The first time I saw the Tapestry it was still hanging up in an upstairs room at the old lace-making school across from the Bayeux cathedral, just as it was in 1966. It was moved into its own climate-controlled and spookily-lit vault in the 1980s.

I hope to be back in Bayeux in 2066, waving my old National Geographic magazine, cheering the **1,000** anniversary of the Norman Conquest.

HOW I BECAME FRENCH 1,2,3

Un

19, alone in Paris, trying out 3 years of high school French for the first time —— that *Parlez-vous* stuff works!

Deux

In my 20s, hitch hiking to the five corners of France — riding shotgun with truck drivers from Alsace to Provence is what I call SIGHT-SEEING.

Trois

Visiting in-laws in Paris in my 30s and my husband's little nephews get giggly when I speak English to them; they say I'm **speaking gibberish!**

My embroidery of
Plains Indian War Horses done in Bayeux Stitch

155

Meet my France

The most common last name in France is **MARTIN** from **St. Martin**, the best-loved of the many patron saints of FRANCE — he is the individual credited with spreading **WINEMAKING** throughout the country.

The FRENCH word for PURR is a beautiful onomatopoeia: **RONRON**

The most famous person in France is the singer known as *the French Elvis*: Johnny Hallyday. Hallyday has been a *huge* star since 1960 performing music that has been described as **defiantly American**. He has sold over 100 million records and has had over 80 books written about him.

IN 1979 I saw Saturday **Night Fever** in PARIS — with French subtitles. I knew the movie had a lot of foul language in it and I wanted to learn how to curse in French so I took a notebook with me into the theater. I still have my notes from that night — it's my only list of the filthiest words I know of in the French language.

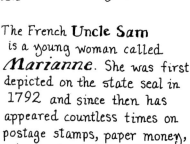

Although the **Poodle** is still the favorite PEDIGREED dog in France **Mutts** are *twice* as popular as *any* purebred.

Virtually unknown in the rest of the (non French-speaking) world he is often called *The biggest rock star you've never heard of.*

French toast in France is called *pain perdue lost bread* because you use stale (*lost*) bread to make it.

The French **Uncle Sam** is a young woman called *Marianne*. She was first depicted on the state seal in 1792 and since then has appeared countless times on postage stamps, paper money, coins, and paintings. The statue of Marianne that adorns every town hall is updated every other decade using the most beautiful woman in France as the model.

The words to the **French National Anthem** are so VIOLENT that many parents refuse to let their **children** sing it.

JENNIFER, a name that is considered *peculiar* in France, had a sudden burst in popularity there in **1985** when it became the **no. 1** name given to baby girls born that year. The reason: an American sitcom called **HART to HART** had become popular on French TV. The female lead, played by Stefanie Powers, was named *Jennifer.*

ACCORDING TO my Francophone first husband, who learned how to speak American during our marriage, the **MOST FUN** word to say in the English language is **TEAPOT**. Short and full of hard consonants, it is a *very* un-FRENCH word that amused him to no end.

MORLAIX town motto:
IF THEY BITE YOU, BITE THEM.
This sounds hilarious in French. (The French have a strange sense of humor.)

There are 14 towns in FRANCE with 2-letter names. Y is the only town with just one. The 82 residents of Y call themselves: Ypsiloniens.

BERGUES In a nation with approx. 40 municipally run PAWNSHOPS the one here has the distinction of being the OLDEST PAWNSHOP in FRANCE (founded 1630).

●Y

●EU
●RY

BAYEUX

Sites of the feuding Cheese Museums in the towns of LIVAROT, VIMOUTIERS, & CAMEMBERT

BOUZY
● It's pronounced "BOOZY" and it's in the heart of CHAMPAGNE COUNTRY.

LE FAOUET
The most isolated town in FRANCE - the people here spoke an ancient Celtic dialect until the 1950s, when French finally became commonly used.

CITY of GOD the FRYING PANS
(Villedieu-Les-Poêles)
See the Frying Pan Museum here in the town famous (since the 12th century) for you know what.

AUXERRE
Famous for being the MOST AVERAGE town in FRANCE

MULHOUSE
has a Museum of Electricity.

The Lion of BELFORT●
is the Masterpiece sculpture by the guy who made the STATUE of LIBERTY.

CASTLE of COMBOURG
Haunted since the 14th century by the ghost of a CAT

BOURGES
Famous for being almost in the EXACT CENTER of FRANCE

The medieval Gothic Cathedral here in SEMUR-en-AUXOIS has ESCARGOT (a regional delicacy) carved into the stonework.

The people of FOUGERES say their town has the prettiest name in FRANCE (in french, fougeres means fern).

HAUTERIVES A mailman in 1879 started to collect the interesting rocks he found on his delivery route 33 years later he had enough rocks to build a CASTLE here.

VALENCE
Home of the largest Shoe Museum in the World

LAGUIOLE
Famous for making the World's best CORKSCREWS

A GIANT CHAIR here, in the middle of nowhere.

CASTLENAUDARY
Famous for its secret recipe for a cake called the Alleluia

●On average ORANGE is the HOTTEST town in FRANCE.

Oô

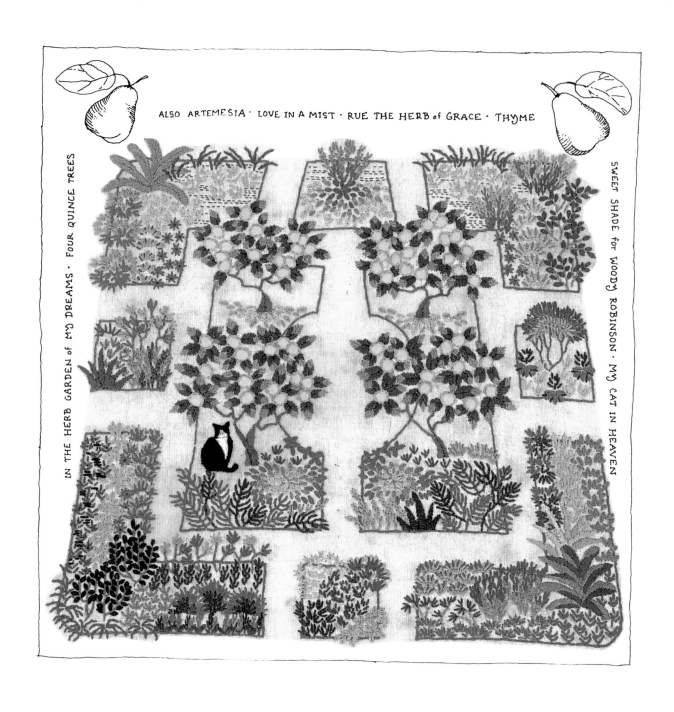

ALSO ARTEMESIA · LOVE IN A MIST · RUE THE HERB of GRACE · THYME

IN THE HERB GARDEN of MY DREAMS · FOUR QUINCE TREES

SWEET SHADE for WOODY ROBINSON · MY CAT IN HEAVEN

opposite page   In honor of the wild quince tree in my Village,
this is everything I know about QUINCE.

OCTOBER is QUINCE month

QUINCE
The neglected autumn pome

Quinces were once common in American gardens, especially in New England. QUINCE was at the height of its popularity with Europeans when they came to settle the new world ~ Quince pastries and preserves were favorites in all the colonies.

THE GOLDEN LOVE APPLE
GIVEN BY PARIS to APHRODITE
leading to the downfall of TROY

The QUINCE fragrance, similar to ripe apples and pears *but* more complex ~ with hints of **tropical** fruits such as pineapple and guava ~ A few quinces in a bowl will perfume an entire room.

WILD QUINCE (ABOVE) come from forgotten gardens that have been naturalized to the country side

Today the QUINCE survives only as an ornamental tree at the edge of ORCHARDS

THE original MARMALADE from the **Roman** MELIMELUM means: QUINCE PRESERVED IN HONEY

QUINCE JAM

Combine 2½ pounds of QUINCE with 6 cups of sugar, bring to a slow boil over medium heat. Skim and ladle into warm, clean half-pint jars and store in a cool cupboard for a year and a half.

NATIVE TO WESTERN ASIA

where it has a LONG HISTORY of cultivation THE QUINCE was brought to **EUROPE** in the MIDDLE AGES where the scent of QUINCES was GREATLY APPRECIATED. Taste for QUINCE declined in the 20th century because it is not suited for fresh consumption.

THE *Fruit* is hard, rather dry, and quite sour when raw, but has *flavors* that are activated by slow cooking. THE PALE FLESH turns color during preparation ~ it deepens into a delicate **coral** or a rich **ruby** red.

Letter to the Editor:

It is music to my ears to know that the leaf blowing machines that invaded our Village in the past decade are going to be restrained to keep our Village a pleasant place to live away from the hustle bustle of New York City.

For years I have lamented the invasion of these monstrous machines mostly because of the noise that drives us all indoors. It is evident that with modern technology home owners have become accustomed to perfect green lawns. The new law to ban the use of these blowers will help us recognize that we need to give up some perfection in order to live peacefully in a quiet Village.

Sincerely,
Mrs. James

Coyote Summer

It's October but suddenly it feels like August. A shift in the upper winds of the jet stream, a **weather singularity**, sends a *Bermuda High* up north to the Long Island Sound with heat from the **tropics**.

Temperatures climb way above normal. It's lazy, hazy, and hot the slow breeze rustles flame-colored leaves, loosens a mellow ripening flavor into the air. It reminds us of traveling light. Of the taste of vanilla tea. Of conversations in low tones, meandering walks in and out of the shade, of phonograph music floating through open windows. It reminds us that what is here today will be gone **tomorrow.**

The **SOUL** needs air, *A WIDE SWEEP* and **frequent change** of it.

Nathaniel Hawthorne, *House of the Seven Gables*, 1851

Life consists of wildness. The MOST ALIVE is the *Wildest*.

Henry David Thoreau, *Walking*, 1857

Coyote Things

Unexplained noises in the night

The sigh you hear in certain kinds of wind

Of all my cats, WINSTON has the eyes of a coyote

Comets

Quarks

The Letter X

Sideburns

Good Luck Charms

The darker shades of Red

The things you find in the pockets of a jacket you
    haven't worn in a year

A scuffle in a pile of leaves when there's not
    any animal or bird in sight

The wild longing to run away, change your name,
    prowl with the trickster

Anything that makes you want to dance

November

The oak trees are letting loose all their acorns. It's called **throwing mast** and those big old oak trees in the Village are doing just that - they *throw* their acorns, aiming for the cars parked under their boughs, setting off their anti-theft alarms. When I've been thwacked on the head, once or twice, it sure felt as if that *mast* was thrown on purpose.

Another thing about oak trees: from a single oak leaf you can deduce an entire FALL landscape.

Family of Wild Turkeys in the Village

This family of wild turkeys was spotted several times this week in the Village. Neighbors have counted as many as 8 turkeys, usually seen in the early morning.

When you catch your first whiff of something in the air that isn't related to living things, you know that the first frost is near. Leaves, grass, flowers – you know what they smell like. **This is different**. It's the scent of cold stone walls and ice vapor, it's the terrible aroma of unfinished business from last December. It smells like nothingness, silence, and deep black nights. **Uh-oh**, you think: *Winter*. Am I ready for this?

NOVEMBER is the GOOD~BYE Month

NOVEMBER thins the year out. The Earth becomes more transparent daily, as every leaf and flower and fruit falls away out of sight. By the end of the month the harvest will be gone, disappeared. It will be **wide open** from here to Spring, infinite void through every shorn tree branch and denuded garden all the way clear to the horizon. It's wide open for a stiff wind to blow in any soul that might want to visit from the other side – that's why the **Druids** called NOVEMBER 1 **All Soul's Day**.

All Soul's Day was the day when the veil between the two worlds, *this* one and the *spirit* one, was particularly thin and spirits could use that transparency to take a stroll from their world to ours. *I get that*.

November is all about this world wasting away, vanishing and about **US** getting used to the nothingness, used to saying GOOD-BYE.

NOVEMBER gives you a good look at what's been hiding behind **Summer**. And it's empty out there. **And I don't like it one bit**. I *should* be welcoming the clearing away of the year as it empties towards December's simplicity, **simplicity** being good and pure and all. On a good day *I get that*.

But this is not a good day. It's rainy and cold and I haven't gotten used to the empty look of the world and I'm not ready to cross over to the **Winter Side**.

It is November, and I have the blues.

November 1

November started off with a thin fog this morning, mixing with the sugary-sweet smell left over from last night, the scent from so many candles baking the insides of all those Halloween pumpkin jack-o-lanterns. My birthday is just two months away and in my opinion, November is not too early to start dreading it. It is November, and I have the blues.

November 2

This morning there was the smell of frost in the air. It was sharp, cold, grey. November.

November 6

It rained yesterday but it's warm this morning. The streets are shiny and full of fallen leaves – so pretty. And the air is sweet with the smell of Fall's wet, herbal warmth.

November 10

A hard rain today, muddy, sorrowful, and cold. Technically November isn't an especially rainy month, but it *is* the *soggiest* month of the year because nothing dampens and darkens the spirit more than **November Rain.**

November 12

Sun set at 4:46 PM today. The twilight was muzzy and dim, like light shining under dark water.

November 13

The coffee kiosk at the train station put out its WINTER MENU today. Now there's Hot Spiced Cider and Hot Chocolate ($1.00) for the morning commute.

November 15

The first part of Fall is over, the first **7** weeks after the Autumnal Equinox during which the trees shed exactly half their leaves. The second half of Fall only lasts a week or two. That's how long it takes the November wind and rain to strip the trees bare.

November 18

Sunday and rain. A bad combination. The rain makes me feel dreary and Sundays always make me feel bluesy. So I spent the afternoon straightening out my jewelry box and sorting out my rock souvenirs.

November 20

November needs soup, lots and lots of it. Tonight I made potato-broccoli. I'm dreaming of the time when there will be soups for every Winter day of the week: tomato, black bean, cabbage, and carrot, pea, and best of all – cream of celery.

November 25

Cold, dark, and drizzly all day.

November 29

Today it rained all day. This is the worst rain of the year, the November rain that wants to be snow. It fell heavy and hard, and took the last leaves off the trees. It feels like the end of everything.

November 30

Something new this morning: **ICE,** there in the frozen puddles of yesterday's rain. They say that comets are the oldest bits of the Universe, the last remnants from the Big Bang. Those comets are balls of dirt and ice. So this is what stardust looks like here on Earth — a puddle of November.

Good-bye
Good-bye
Good-bye

November 15
Half-way Fall

November 29
Fall all gone

I have the
Good-bye
Blues

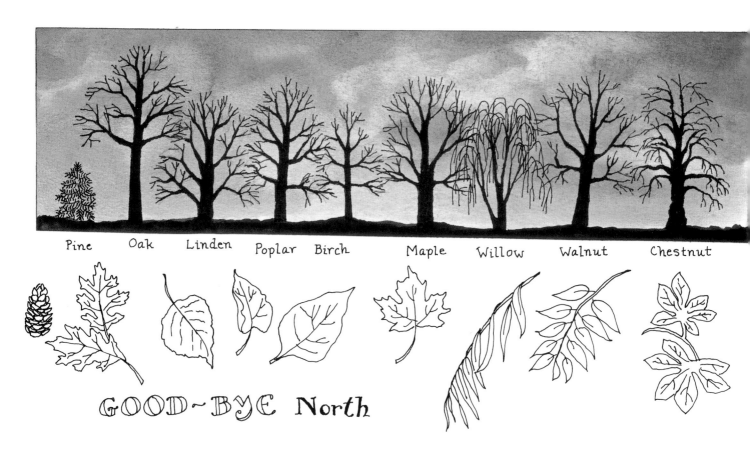

Pine   Oak   Linden   Poplar Birch   Maple   Willow   Walnut   Chestnut

GOOD~BYE North

November on the edges of town

There's Chester Park, the northern-most neighborhood in the Village, with all its streets named after trees. And there's the Founder's Manor far to the South, a water-front public property with Nature Walks along the Long Island Sound. November hits hardest at these two **garden spots**.

You can walk **North** and collect a leaf from every street and while you're at it, imagine what it was like here, in 1890. That's the year before the huge old Standen estate was divided up into lots (now there's 165 houses here) and became a Homestead Association named for the 21st President of the United States.

You can walk **South** and recollect our old Lords of the Manor by roaming the last nine acres of the original 9,166-acre patch of New World that our Founder purchased in 1654. The Founder paid the native Siwanoy Indians some "bits of [English] money" along with a few shirts, coats, axes, guns, kettles, and cider for the land.

The Lords and the Siwanoys and their descendants disappeared long ago from the Village, and facing the Chester Park Green, where the original stone steps to the entrance to the old estate still stand, there's a Sears Catalog house -- one of the 100,000 pre-fab homes that the retailer sold from 1914 to 1940.

It is November and nothing lasts forever.

On Saturday the Garden Club held its November Presentation at the Founder's Manor. Nine daughters of members were escorted by their fathers and presented to the Governing Board of the Garden Club, its membership, and guests.

The Debutante Reception is a tradition inaugurated by the late Mrs. Francis Ludsworth in 1959. She believed it was appropriate to intro—duce the Garden Club's young ladies at the Founder's Manor, which is listed in the National Register of Historic Places. In 1914 the property came under the aegis of the Garden Club, whose members raised the funds for the restoration of the Manor and the construction of the herb garden and the formal gardens.

Debutantes: Margret, Laura, Catherine, Kimberly, Christina, Meagan, Carolyn, Katharine, & Sarah.

GOOD~BYE South

173

THE BLUES
The Blahs
THE WEARY DISMALS

Lost in Gloom
Woesome Me's
THE Eternal 3 am of the SOUL

A MEMOIR of BLUE in Five Minuscule Chapters

1. BLEU

Ennui, they say, is the price of sophistication. And no one pays a higher price than **Parisians**. In Paris, the most sophisticated city on Earth, they call **the blues**: *le cafard*, "the cockroach". It was one of the most useful phrases I learned when I first came to live in Paris. "*J'ai le cafard*," I'd sigh, the existential apathy oozing out of my 23-year-old self: *I have the cockroach.*"

Le cafard goes back to 1860, back to the **FRENCH FOREIGN LEGION** — *le cafard* was military slang used only by **Legion** soldiers (who were mostly convicted criminals, slightly insane, and/or social misfits) who had served in the Sahara Desert where the terrible isolation and harsh weather & living conditions caused an almost universal DESERT MADNESS they called *le cafard*. Discharged soldiers brought the term back with them to Paris, along with their favorite beverage, a new liquid drug called *absinthe*.

At first the only people crazy enough to drink this highly potent, addictive liquor were the disreputable **Legionnaires**. But by the 1880s absinthe drinking had become **très chic** among slumming members of high society, who no doubt picked up some new slang to go with their new buzz. They had **the cockroach** — and didn't they feel deliciously *avant-garde* every time they said it?

Absinthe was finally outlawed in 1915. But *le cafard* lives on:

In the spector of the crazed souls of the French Foreign Legion, the desolation of the bleak African desert, the woozy hangover of an illicit psychoactive alcoholic poison, all that **ennui** summed up in one bug: *le cafard*.

Of course Parisians wouldn't have anything as ordinaire as **the blues.**

2. LAZAWARD

The bluest thing known to the ancients was a ROCK that they reckoned was a chip off the celestial firmament, so they called it the *stone* (lapis) *of heaven* (lazuli). **Lazuli** is from the Arabic word for a specific shade of blue, the "heavenly sky blue" they called **Lazaward**.

The Arabs also had a word for the dreaded cold wind that blows off the Sahara in the Winter months, a wind so vicious that it hurls clouds of desert sand across the Atlantic Ocean into South America. They call this *haram*, this *evil thing*, the **Harmattan**. *This* is the wind that bedeviled the French Foreign Legion, that accounted so much for the **misery** that they called **le cafard** — the DESERT MADNESS.

In my one-room hovel in the capital city of Niamey in the old French colony of Niger, I'd close up my shutters and shroud my food and books and clothes with sheets. But nothing could prevent the **Harmattan** from infiltrating the finest thread count, leaving a powdery layer of grit on everything.

What kept me sane in the season of DESERT MADNESS was the nearby bar of the **TERMINUS** hotel (named for the *terminal* of a railroad that was never built), where I would find shelter — and order some ice-cold heavenly rocks plunked into a full glass of Cinzano Russo.

3. BLAE

Robert Lewis Stevenson wrote that his native Scottish language was uniquely rich in terms that conjured the Winter winds that chilled the psyche of his people. For example, there was **Blae**, he said (a word that means both *blue-grey* and *livid*), that could make him shiver just *hearing* it.

The blue-grey skies of Scotland were most livid, in my memory, over an empty cold beach on the west coast. It wasn't Winter, but I was chilled through and through, wrapped tightly in a too-thin jacket against the wind that blew off the cliffs to the North Atlantic sunset. **Snell**, the air was; **nirly** and **scowthering** too.

Uisge, the Scots word for the *water of life* (also known as **whisky**) is what can warm a soul on a **Blae** day. Just a sip, and I am back on that Highland beach, tasting the sea spray and breathing the livid air; and if the memory of a heartbreak or two appears

It is but a heartbreak of air
That lingers on the shoreline there.

4. AZUR

English is one of the few languages that has a separate word for a certain shade of light red: we call it **Pink**. What we *don't* have is a separate word for its corollary in blue, a delicate shade which the Italians call **Azzuro**. The French borrowed this word to describe the luscious light blue color of the Mediterranean waters on the south coast, the **Côte d'Azur**.

But the winds of that coast are not so pretty. In Winter and again in Spring, the south of France is battered by a cold **50**-mile-an-hour wind that the locals say will drive men and animals mad. The howling, parching, enervating wind is the master of bad moods; in the local dialect they call it *the Master*: **Le Mistral**.

I was in the town of Roquefort the first time I stood in the swath of the **Mistral**. I stood in the lane behind the farmhouse where my first French boyfriend was starting a commune and I turned towards the wind, hoping it would blow every iota of my American suburban upbringing out of me.

5. SAPPHIRE

The Biblical stone was originally called **Sapir** in Hebrew, which was translated into **Sapphire** around 90 CE. The color most associated with sapphire is blue, but the gem actually comes in many hues – the most famous "fancy" color being **red**. Such a sapphire is better known as a **ruby**.

The Bible Lands are also prone to a **red** hot wind blown up north from the Sahara and then eastwards across to the Levant. Called **SHARAV** in Hebrew (*for burning heat*) and **SHARKIYE** in Arabic (*for easterly*) such a wind is better known by its European name: **Sirocco**.

Temperatures can soar to 120°F during a sirocco in the Levant. Not that it ever bothered me ⌇ I loved the heat. I also loved the way the sirocco filled the air with dust and sand particles that refracted light from the setting sun, the way that light shone off the waters of the Sea of Galilee in colors I've never seen before, colors I didn't know the names of.

left: Candy
right: Honey

Get Some Comfort Cats

Old cats will make you happy. Especially if you adopt them TOGETHER when they end up at a shelter in their old age after a lifetime in each other's company.

The 8th Pillar of Wisdom

I learned my lesson in the Sahara- when dressing for the elements, keep it simple: no buttons, bows, or belts. Think of this **November Wrap** as a **caftan** for the **cold desert**, with pockets for carrying the drawing pens & lip gloss, paté knives and cork screws that no desert nomad would be without. O.K., O.K., it's only a bathrobe,
    but Lawrence of Arabia would approve.

On November 16 give or take a week:
Set your alarm for 4:30 AM. Put your Winter coat on over your jammies and take a lawn chair up to the roof. Look to the North, to the constellation Leo. There will be a shower of shooting stars falling down from the sky — this is the wake of the Temple-Tuttle comet that zooms through our solar system every 33 years, scattering bits of stardust onto Earth. Imagine that you are in the heavens, looking down on this spectacle. Imagine how your blues look from such a great height. Allow yourself a **SIGH.** Go back to bed. When you wake up, don't take November so seriously.

Comforts of the Blues

The ancient Egyptians believed that Lapis lazuli's heavenly color could counteract the wily spirits of darkness. The Babylonians wore Lapis as a cure for melancholy. William Butler Yeats wrote a poem about it: I knew the poem before I'd ever laid eyes on Lapis Lazuli. I felt **rich** the day I bought my November necklace.

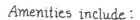

The Living Room November Resort

Amenities include:

A good lamp for lighting up the 4 o'clock twilight

Proximity to the kitchen (hot water for tea, ice cubes for the Lagavulin)

A remote control for the radio so you can turn it off when NPR starts playing jazz

Height & weight-appropriate easy chair with foot stool to achieve the perfect ergonomic supine position

No reason to move for the five hours it takes to read a Wodehouse novel

Collect Autobiographical Tchotchkes

Surely you can think of *something,* can't you?

December

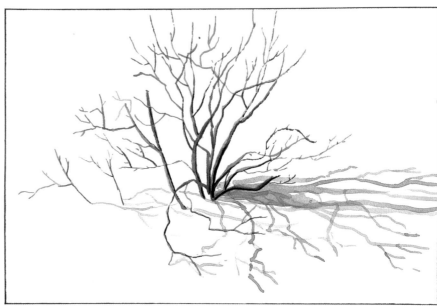

Now is the time of fresh starts

This is the season that makes everything new. There is a longstanding rumor that **Spring** is the time of renewal, but that's only if you ignore the depressing clutter and din of the season. All that flowering and budding and birthing — the messy *youthfulness* of Spring actually verges on **SQUALOR**. Spring is too busy, too full of itself, too much like a **20-year-old** to be the best time for reflection, re-grouping, and starting fresh.

For *that* you need December. You need to have lived through the mindless biological imperatives of your life (to bud, and flower, and show off) before you can see that a landscape of new fallen snow is THE REAL YOU. December has the clarity, the simplicity, and the silence you need for the best **FRESH START** of your life.

DECEMBER is the MOVING ON Month

The antidote to November's Blues is December White. A blanket of new snow clears away the past and gives you a view of what is on the other side of these cold days: *A New Year!* Brand new! For YOU! What a surprise!

It's like the wind chimes on the Old Barge Canal on the edge of the Village. They are there all year — 40, 50, maybe a hundred wind chimes — in the branches of the trees that surround the drawbridge there. Robert, the drawbridge keeper for the past 30 years, planted all those trees (he says the trees talk to him, keep him company on his solitary vigils for the few barges that still navigate this far inland from the Long Island Sound). And for 30 years he's made wind chimes out of old gears, springs, car keys, and flanges, draped in the trees like metallic Spanish moss. For most of the year the wind chimes are buried, unseen, deep in the foliage ⌇ but at this time of year they are revealed, exposed, IN PLAIN SIGHT. Like the New Year that is also now in view, the wind chimes are **December's gift**.

The Inuit people of the Frozen North DON'T have 50 words for snow. I looked it up. They actually have very *few* words for snow — no more than 6 or 7, along the lines of **powder, slush, drifting snow, packed powder, blizzard,** and **corn snow**. One word that they *do* have is **KAVISERDLAQ**, which is *frozen snow that's been pock-marked by rain*. But because the word **KAVISERDLAQ** is derived from the Inuit word that means "fish scales", linguists don't count it as a SNOW word, they count it as a FISH SCALE word. This hardly seems fair.

On the LONG ISLAND SOUND we have fish scale snow too. We also have **Cottontail** snow,[1] **Angel food cake batter** snow[2], and **Heirloom wedding lace** snow[3].

[1] This is also known as SEA SNOW: when moist air from the South flows up North and meets a cold front over land the result is a frozen fog, floating in the air like a suspended flurry.
[2] Or, SEA ICE (rare): ice that forms in salt water.
[3] Commonly known as FAST ICE: formed on the shoreline, made up of breaking waves' sea spray that has frozen in place as an icy, foaming semi-solid.

December 1

The coldest air mass this season is heading our way and words that we'd almost forgotten are coming back into the weather forecast: **wind chill, frostbite, frigid.**

December 2

On my walk to the library today I picked up the first welcome sign of the season, a tiny red mitten on the sidewalk, this Winter's first addition to my Lost and Found of miniature (children's) mittens.

December 3

Christmas trees, fresh cut from upstate forests, here and on sale on the Village green.

December 7

The first snow! As pure as a new beginning. No wonder I love this time of year.

December 8

Toesy. That's my new word for the tip-toe delight in being snug at home and wearing new slippers on the first *of many* bitter cold, snowy nights.

December 11

Plenty more snow overnight. The morning was bright and blank and infinitely hopeful, as only a new-snow morning can be.

December 12

Wintery Sunsets: fire on the horizon, ice on the roof.

December 14

Now starts the Halcyon Days, the legendary peaceful days when the kingfishers calm the winds to make their nests on the sea waves. The sky here, full of turbulent Winter storm clouds, is the same grey-blue color of kingfisher feathers.

December 18

It's for days like this that I wish we had 50 words for snow, for the snow that fell today, dainty as powdered sugar; and a word for the snow it covered up, old and dirty as used cement. A word, too, for that new-snow smell, of something rare ⌣ like an iced dessert flavored with the petals of an Asian Slipper Orchid.

December 22

Solstice sunrise 7:15, sun set at 4:30.

December 23

Real mistletoe for sale at the florist's today! $4.00 for a twig of the magic berries.

December 26

Row boats are laying scattered on the cold shores of the Long Island Sound, pulled out of the water for the Winter, scattered on the beach like broken souvenirs of Summer.

December 28

A hard rain, then an all-day blizzard. I watched the snow obliterate the landscape while sipping lots of Assam chai tea which, from now on, will always taste like December to me.

December 30

What snow! I had to go out in it – the snow came up to my knees and I had to laugh, staggering in the drifts as if walking were a skill that I hadn't yet mastered on this planet.

December 31

Today I took a walk along the shore of the Long Island Sound. It is cold and still, frozen in time. There's only me, the sea gulls, a few abandoned boats, and the tide to witness the passing of the old year. The sea gulls will stay. But the tide and I know: it's time to move on.

An estimated 1,000,000,000,000,000,000,000,000,000,000,000,000 (one undecillion)
SNOWFLAKES have fallen on the planet Earth.

Snow is white because the 6-sided snow crystal refracts every color of the spectrum equally, blending all the colors in a beam of light. All those colors together make white.

There is a lot of space between the loosely stacked snowflakes of new-fallen snow, like a sponge, absorbing sound waves. This is why there really *is* a hush on a snowy day.

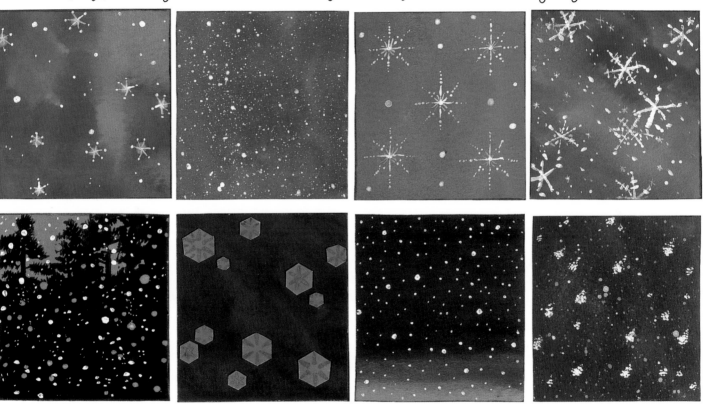

DIAMOND DUST is the kind of snow that falls in very COLD, very DRY conditions.

SNOW tastes like watermelon. Put a snowball in your freezer until July and compare!

KINDS OF SNOW

Snow that you can smell is about to fall on a cold, quiet day.

Snow that lights up an otherwise depressing afternoon.

It is after dinner and you go out the back door to take the garbage out and discover that the alley ① is covered with a light snowfall that you didn't expect ∽ and ② has small animal footprints down the length of it from a wild creature that had been there *moments* before you - this is TWICE SECRET snow.

Deep, heavy, icy SNOW DAY SNOW that waits until Sunday night to fall. That's my favorite kind of snow.

Drifting snow
Sledding snow
Snow that smoothes things over

Snow that glitters at sunrise
Snow that sparkles in the dark of night
Blue - in - the - shadows snow.

This past weekend, with the new snow that fell on Friday, snowmen builders in the Village were out in force. Our previous community of snow people were delighted by the 12-inch snow fall that gave them so many new friends.

✳ ✳ ✳

One sad footnote to the snowmen building news: missing is a child's scarf that was on a snowman near Highbrook Avenue. The scarf has sentimental value (it was a gift from Santa). If the scarf is found in a snowbank or even after the snow melts, please call us here at the Village Weekly.

✳ ✳ ✳

However, the good snow elves have also been out in force. Judy Rose wants to thank whoever it was who shoveled her sidewalk and driveway on the day of the big storm.

Shop window on Wolf's Lane

Santa and Gumby Spread Holiday Cheer

The Village Volunteer Fire Company continued its tradition of helping Gumby and Santa Claus make some early holiday deliveries. Riding on two antique fire trucks, Gumby and Santa Claus delighted many Village families with a surprise visit and candy canes aplenty.

Snowman on Ancon Avenue & Peter G. with his fort on Fowler Avenue

DECEMBER
in the Village

Wind chimes at the Old Barge Canal

On the edge of the Village, near the exit off U.S. Route 1, surrounded by run-down warehouses and auto body repair shops, near the cemetery where the Continental Army of 1776 buried fallen enemy Hessians, at the farthest inland passage of the tides from the Long Island Sound ⟨~⟩ is the place where ROBERT BORZACCHINI (bridge keeper for 30+ years) says:

"God put me here to straighten out this part of Earth."

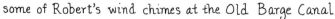

some of Robert's wind chimes at the Old Barge Canal

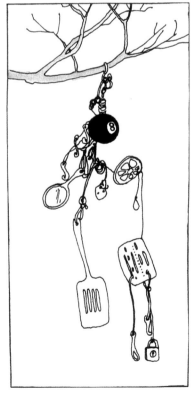

above: The drawbridge and bridge house on the **Old Barge Canal**

This is the corner of the Village I call
ROBERT WORLD

First, he planted trees: oriental elm, corkscrew willow, Norway maple, Oswego orange, a Tree of Heaven. When they grew tall, he draped them with wind chimes he made with found bits of automatic transmissions, old toys, rusted hardware, household trash, and broken down appliances that litter the banks of the canal. He ploughed and paved terraces and pathways, setting shards of colored glass into wet cement and arranging pretty stones to decorate the bare dirt. He nailed a hundred old fans onto the utility poles to catch the winds that blow our way from the Southern Hemisphere.

  Most people don't see any of this. They drive by so fast in their cars that they don't notice these "features of wonderment" that Robert has put here for their benefit.

  My walk to the drawbridge takes 15 minutes. I will watch the water flow into the canal with Robert, and we will talk of many things: ships, and shoes, the secret language of trees, Martian house guests, and rock collecting on Mt. Vesuvius. We will drink hot tea, and Robert will say to me, over and over,

  "Life is a very interesting place to visit."

HALCYON DAYS are the 14 days of **tranquility** in December that are caused, according to legend, by the power of the **Kingfisher** to calm the seas so that she can build her nest on the still surface of the water.

TROUBLED WATERS

Kingfisher grey is the color of the day. But all is not well in the Village by the sea.

I came to this Village because I wanted to quit the waywardness of the wanderer's life. And the longer I stay put here, settled in with cats, leases, utility bills and sentimental attachments, the more I hope that everything will **always stay the same**.

But the more I want things to stay the same, the more things seem to change **every day**. It's an illusion, I know — the slower you live, the faster the world passes you by; the faster the normal *inevitable* rate of change appears. And by staying put, as I have, I haven't had much practice in the art of change. My ability to **adapt** is disappearing.

The wind chimes at the Old Barge Canal are gone. The thousands of found objects that used to hang from the trees on the banks of the canal like a beautiful filigree – **GONE**. Robert, the drawbridge keeper on the canal, told me that a county bureaucrat had become so infuriated at the sight of what he called the "garbage in the trees" that he sent a maintenance crew to tear all the wind chimes out. I had barely absorbed the spitefulness of such destruction when Robert informed me that the crew was coming back later in the day to finish the "clean up" on the banks of the Old Barge Canal by *chopping down all the trees.*

For 30 years Robert worked to beautify this patch of Earth and now it's all going to vanish. I am heartsick. But Robert, being more forward-looking, is not as perturbed by these sudden changes as I am. He already has plans to re-build his *features of* **wonderment** in a new, secret location; I am left to **resent** and **mourn** the changes at the Old Barge Canal **on my own**.

I never used to be like this.

Halcyon, the Mythical Bird

The **Belted Kingfisher** is the only kingfisher found throughout North America. The birds have a deep bluish-grey color, with the female having a cinnamon-colored belt across her white belly.

I've always wanted to drive a jeep to Tierra del Fuego. I still fancy a honeymoon in France ᔐ that is, if I ever get married again (at midnight, on the Strip in Las Vegas, with Elvis in the house). I've never been to Scotland in the Winter. I've never seen New Orleans in the Summer, –– or a Kingfisher either. I'm going to be 50 years old someday and I've never touched a tiger.

These boats, waiting out the Winter on the shore of the Long Island Sound, are all the things I haven't done.
Yet.

It's time to row my boat
Gently down the stream.
Snow is falling
Night is calling
Life is but a Winter dream.

It's time for this Homebody to hit the road.

Sunsets
on the
Long
Island
Sound

The LONG NIGHT MOON

The December
FULL MOON
also known as the
MOON BEFORE YULE

is the **BRIGHTEST**
moon of the year
because
it is the *closest*
moon to EARTH
and because
it rides **HIGHER**
in the sky than any
other **FULL MOON**

Welcome~in the Winter night...
for The night of talk and storytelling.

EDNA ST. VINCENT MILLAY

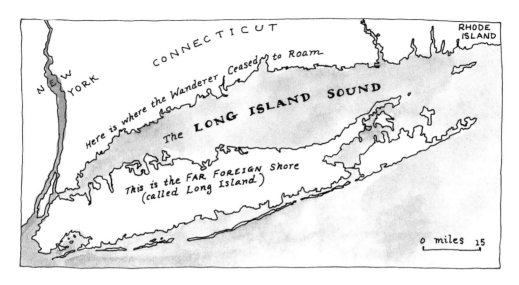

EPILOGUE

THINGS CHANGE. I couldn't stay put forever.

My friend Andy told me that if I came to his party (in the Spring of 2003) I'd meet some cute guys. Otherwise I probably wouldn't have dragged myself all the way down to New York City on a weeknight.

He was right. Five minutes after checking my coat I made the acquaintance of James Andrew Stone, who I married (after a decent interval) in Las Vegas, on the Strip, at midnight. Elvis pronounced us Husband and Wife. I finally got to wear the vintage black cocktail dress I'd been saving for *just* such an occasion.

I had to leave my beloved Village to go live in my husband's 100-year-old house *way* across the water, on the far side of the Long Island Sound. Exactly ten years after my last moving day I found myself once again starting a new life, in a new home, hoping that this would be the place where I could stay put forever.

The more things change, the more they stay the same.

And that's a whole other story.

ACKNOWLEDGMENTS

A traveler never forgets the first time that she truly feels like a wanderer, at large in the world, cut loose from her hometown frames of reference. For me, that day came at the Canterbury Youth Hostel in 1976, when Sue from Rhodesia let me tag along with her for a long walk through the town. I tried so hard to be nonchalant. But it was a heart-pounding *thrill* for me, to be hanging out with a real, live *foreigner*, and she even let me take a picture of her in her dashiki in front of the famous half-timbered Weavers' Houses. Thank you, Sue, for giving this hick her first taste of world citizenship.

To Gary Robinson: We'll always have Bastille Day.

Wendy Hesher, a fellow traveler from Paris to the Peace Corps to the suburbs, is the person I trade road stories with. We'll always have Africa in our twenties.

As for staying put, there's no better place than the Village of Pelham on the Long Island Sound. And I highly recommend Barbara and John Moran, Lee and Dave Clark, Scott Stiefvater and Marilyn Stiefvater as neighbors – they are the kind of people who will feed your cats and lend you books and drop in for tea just when you'd most like some company, and what they don't know about what goes on in our Village isn't worth knowing.

There's a downside to staying put. It's called "Getting a Real Job." But I'm thankful to have gotten real friends in spite of the circumstances. Beryl Bush continues to come up with scathingly brilliant ideas. Bennett Degen is a stand-up guy and I'm glad I know him. Andy Hort and the Rema Hort Mann Foundation: I celebrate you every May 1.

I've been keeping diaries since I was nineteen so when it came to writing this book I didn't have to make anything up. But I did have to check facts. Arthur Scinta, Pelham architectural historian, helped me with my enquiries about Village history. Karen Ghezzi, Library Associate at the Earl J. Wooster High School in Reno, Nevada, dug up the old yearbooks and confirmed my suspicions that my Class of 1973 was the *coolest ever*. Elizabeth Peters at Bloomsbury showed me how this whole "publishing" thing works with kindly perseverance and Cather-esque clarity.

To Rolly Karlen, playwright and relative extraordinaire, thank you for everything.

Before I met James Stone I never thought I'd have much in common with a Grateful Dead *philosophe*. Then I met James Stone. I didn't know what I was missing.

Vivian Swift was born in 1956 in Missoula, Montana. Using the hitch-hiking skills she learned as a high schooler in Alaska, California, and Nevada, she began traveling overseas when she was 19. In between her foreign wanders she has worked as a receptionist, gift shop sales lady, luxury hotel concierge, clothing store manager, book shop clerk, office temp, retail jeweler, auction house executive, and Fabergé expert. She lives on the Long Island Sound.